11-26-40

17.95
70J

ILLEGAL ALIENS

Senior Consulting Editor

Senator Daniel Patrick Moynihan

Consulting Editors

Ann Orlov
Managing Editor, Harvard
Encyclopedia of American
Ethnic Groups

M. Mark Stolarik
*President, The Balch Institute
for Ethnic Studies, Philadelphia*

James F. Watts
*Chairman, History Department,
City College of New York*

The Peoples of North America

ILLEGAL ALIENS

Pierre N. Hauser

CHELSEA HOUSE PUBLISHERS
New York Philadelphia

On the cover: Three undocumented Mexican immigrants huddle in the back of the
false-bottomed truck in which they snuck across the border in June 1948.

CHELSEA HOUSE PUBLISHERS
Editor-in-Chief: Nancy Toff
Executive Editor: Remmel T. Nunn
Managing Editor: Karyn Gullen Browne
Copy Chief: Juliann Barbato
Picture Editor: Adrian G. Allen
Art Director: Maria Epes
Manufacturing Manager: Gerald Levine
Systems Manager: Rachel Vigier

The Peoples of North America
Senior Editor: Sean Dolan

Staff for THE ILLEGAL ALIENS
Copy Editor: Philip Koslow
Deputy Copy Chief: Mark Rifkin
Picture Research: PAR/NYC
Assistant Art Director: Loraine Machlin
Senior Designer: Noreen M. Lamb
Production Manager: Joseph Romano
Production Coordinator: Marie Claire Cebrián
Cover Illustration: Paul Biniasz
Banner Design: Hrana Janto

First Printing

1   3   5   7   9   8   6   4   2

Library of Congress Cataloging-in-Publication Data
Hauser, Pierre N.
  Illegal Aliens/Pierre N. Hauser.
    p. cm.—(The Peoples of North America)
  Summary: Examines the history of undocumented immigration to the United States,
the hardships endured by illegal aliens, their motives in immigrating, and current
efforts to control this situation.
  1. United States—Emigration and immigration—History. 2. United States—Emigration and immigration—Government policy. 3. Aliens, Illegal—United States—History.
4. Aliens, Illegal—Government policy—United States. [1. United States—Emigration
and immigration. 2. Aliens, Illegal.] I. Title. II. Series.
JV6450.H38 1990
325.73—dc20   90-32356
ISBN 0-87754-889-7   CIP
        0-7910-0294-2 (pbk.)   AC

CONTENTS

THE PEOPLES OF NORTH AMERICA

CHELSEA HOUSE PUBLISHERS

A NATION
OF NATIONS

Daniel Patrick Moynihan

The Constitution of the United States begins: "We the People of the United States . . . " Yet, as we know, the United States is not made up of a single group of people. It is made up of many peoples. Immigrants from Europe, Asia, Africa, and Central and South America settled in North America seeking a new life filled with opportunities unavailable in their homeland. Coming from many nations, they forged one nation and made it their own. More than 100 years ago, Walt Whitman expressed this perception of America as a melting pot: "Here is not merely a nation, but a teeming Nation of nations."

Although the ingenuity and acts of courage of these immigrants, our ancestors, shaped the North American way of life, we sometimes take their contributions for granted. This fine series, *The Peoples of North America*, examines the experiences and contributions of the immigrants and how these contributions determined the future of the United States and Canada.

Immigrants did not abandon their ethnic traditions when they reached the shores of North America. Each ethnic group had its own customs and traditions, and each brought different experiences, accomplishments, skills, values, styles of dress, and tastes in food that lingered long after its arrival. Yet this profusion of differences created a singularity, or bond, among the immigrants.

The United States and Canada are unusual in this respect. Whereas religious and ethnic differences have sparked intolerance throughout the rest of the world—from the 17th-century religious wars to the 19th-century nationalist movements in Europe to the near extermination of the Jewish people under Nazi Germany— North Americans have struggled to learn how to respect each other's differences and live in harmony.

Millions of immigrants from scores of homelands brought diversity to our continent. In a mass migration, some 12 million immigrants passed through the waiting rooms of New York's Ellis Island; thousands more came to the West Coast. At first, these immigrants were welcomed because labor was needed to meet the demands of the Industrial Age. Soon, however, the new immigrants faced the prejudice of earlier immigrants who saw them as a burden on the economy. Legislation was passed to limit immigration. The Chinese Exclusion Act of 1882 was among the first laws closing the doors to the promise of America. The Japanese were also effectively excluded by this law. In 1924, Congress set immigration quotas on a country-by-country basis.

Such prejudices might have triggered war, as they did in Europe, but North Americans chose negotiation and compromise instead. This determination to resolve differences peacefully has been the hallmark of the peoples of North America.

The remarkable ability of Americans to live together as one people was seriously threatened by the issue of slavery. It was a symptom of growing intolerance in the world. Thousands of settlers from the British Isles had arrived in the colonies as indentured servants, agreeing to work for a specified number of years on farms or as apprentices in return for passage to America and room and board. When the first Africans arrived in the then-British colonies during the 17th century, some colonists thought that they too should be treated as indentured servants. Eventually, the question of whether the Africans should be viewed as indentured, like the English, or as slaves who could be owned for life, was considered in a Maryland court. The court's calamitous decree held that blacks were slaves bound to lifelong servitude, and so were their children. America went through a time of moral examination and civil war before it finally freed African slaves and their descendants. The principle that all people are created equal had faced its greatest challenge and survived.

Yet the court ruling that set blacks apart from other races fanned flames of discrimination that burned long after slavery was abolished—and that still flicker today. The concept of racism had existed for centuries in countries throughout the world. For instance, when the Manchus conquered China in the 13th century, they decreed that Chinese and Manchus could not intermarry. To impress their superiority on the conquered Chinese, the Manchus ordered all Chinese men to wear their hair in a long braid called a queue.

By the 19th century, some intellectuals took up the banner of racism, citing Charles Darwin. Darwin's scientific studies hypothesized that highly evolved animals were dominant over other animals. Some advocates of this theory applied it to humans, asserting that certain races were more highly evolved than others and thus were superior.

This philosophy served as the basis for a new form of discrimination, not only against nonwhite people but also against various ethnic groups. Asians faced harsh discrimination and were depicted by popular 19th-century newspaper cartoonists as depraved, degenerate, and deficient in intelligence. When the Irish flooded American cities to escape the famine in Ireland, the cartoonists caricatured the typical "Paddy" (a common term for Irish immigrants) as an apelike creature with jutting jaw and sloping forehead.

By the 20th century, racism and ethnic prejudice had given rise to virulent theories of a Northern European master race. When Adolf Hitler came to power in Germany in 1933, he popularized the notion of Aryan supremacy. *Aryan*, a term referring to the Indo-European races, was applied to so-called superior physical characteristics such as blond hair, blue eyes, and delicate facial features. Anyone with darker and heavier features was considered inferior.

Buttressed by these theories, the German Nazi state from 1933 to 1945 set out to destroy European Jews, along with Poles, Russians, and other groups considered inferior. It nearly succeeded. Millions of these people were exterminated.

The tragedies brought on by ethnic and racial intolerance throughout the world demonstrate the importance of North America's efforts to create a society free of prejudice and inequality.

A relatively recent example of the New World's desire to resolve ethnic friction nonviolently is the solution the Canadians found to a conflict between two ethnic groups. A long-standing dispute as to whether Canadian culture was properly English or French resurfaced in the mid-1960s, dividing the peoples of the French-speaking Quebec Province from those of the English-speaking provinces. Relations grew tense, then bitter, then violent. The Royal Commission on Bilingualism and Biculturalism was established to study the growing crisis and to propose measures to ease the tensions. As a result of the commission's recommendations, all official documents and statements from the national government's capital at Ottawa are now issued in both French and English, and bilingual education is encouraged.

The year 1980 marked a coming of age for the United States's ethnic heritage. For the first time, the U.S. Census asked people about their ethnic background. Americans chose from more than 100 groups, including French Basque, Spanish Basque, French Canadian, Afro-American, Peruvian, Armenian, Chinese, and Japanese. The ethnic group with the largest response was English (49.6 million). More than 100 million Americans claimed ancestors from the British Isles, which includes England, Ireland, Wales, and Scotland. There were almost as many Germans (49.2 million) as English. The Irish-American population (40.2 million) was third, but the next largest ethnic group, the Afro-Americans, was a distant fourth (21 million). There was a sizable group of French ancestry (13 million), as well as of Italian (12 million). Poles, Dutch, Swedes, Norwegians, and Russians followed. These groups, and other smaller ones, represent the wondrous profusion of ethnic influences in North America.

Canada, too, has learned more about the diversity of its population. Studies conducted during the French/English conflict showed that Canadians were descended from Ukrainians, Germans, Italians, Chinese, Japanese, native Indians, and Eskimos, among others. Canada found it had no ethnic majority, although nearly half of its immigrant population had come from the British Isles. Canada, like the United States, is a land of immigrants for whom mutual tolerance is a matter of reason as well as principle.

The people of North America are the descendants of one of the greatest migrations in history. And that migration is not over. Koreans, Vietnamese, Nicaraguans, Cubans, and many others are heading for the shores of North America in large numbers. This mix of cultures shapes every aspect of our lives. To understand ourselves, we must know something about our diverse ethnic ancestry. Nothing so defines the North American nations as the motto on the Great Seal of the United States: *E Pluribus Unum*—Out of Many, One.

Two young Mexicans, presumably illegal aliens, cross the U.S. border near Tijuana, Mexico. It is estimated that in the 1980s as many as 10 million immigrants have entered the United States illegally.

THE UNWANTED IMMIGRANTS

On a warm afternoon in September 1986, 46 young Mexican men gathered on a grassy hill overlooking the Rio Grande. Across the river lay the United States, where they planned to immigrate. They hoped to find jobs, start families, put down roots, as millions of others had done. It was a classic American story. But these men faced a different challenge. They planned to cross the border secretly—and illegally.

The men waited nervously. To pass the time, they played cards and swapped stories about the small farming villages they had left behind. Sometimes they fell silent and stared below at the surface of the swiftly moving river. All the men were dressed in a manner that they hoped would conceal their national origin. They wore cowboy boots, blue jeans, and T-shirts printed with English words. Each carried a change of clothes, a hat, a pair of sandals, and some dried meat—all stuffed into a woven fiber bag called a *costale*.

At last, at about three o'clock in the morning, the men stirred. Their *coyote* (guide) had finally appeared. He was a Mexican. He greeted them tersely and then instructed them to remove their pants and shoes. They did so, putting them in plastic bags that the coyote provided. Then they followed him down to the river. They waded into the chilly waters. It was an eerie feeling, paddling into the darkness.

The current was strong, and the men struggled to keep from being dragged far downstream. Eventually they touched shore. They quickly dressed and began a long walk upriver, trudging as silently as possible. All around them was the desert, alive with nighttime noises. After two hours, they reached a ditch. Here they must wait, the coyote told them, until their next guide arrived. Then the coyote collected $50 from each man and slipped into the Texas brush.

It was noon when the second coyote appeared. He led the men to a dusty fire road, where a U-Haul truck stood, its metal cargo door lifted open. The coyote told the men to climb inside; the truck would convey them to their final destination. The men were amazed. There were 46 of them, the space inside the truck seemed cramped, and Chicago, Illinois, where they were headed, was many hours away. How could they stay cooped inside once the desert began to boil with heat? But they had no choice. They must either pile in or troop back to Mexico, $50 poorer. The men crammed into the back of the truck, and the coyote slammed the door. But first he told them that when they reached Chicago they would each have to pay an additional $100.

Inside, it was pitch-black. The 46 men elbowed and jostled, trying to get comfortable, and the truck pushed across the sizzling Texas desert. As the men had feared, the metal walls that contained them became a magnet for the sun's rays and quickly heated up. It was well above 100 degrees Fahrenheit. No fresh air filtered in. For a toilet, there was only a plastic bucket and some paper towels. Some men fainted. Others gasped wildly for breath. A few yelled and pounded their fists on the walls of the truck.

Finally, the vehicle pulled over. The driver came around, but he did not open the cargo door. He stood outside and called in to the men. It was impossible to open the truck, he said. He had no key. They must wait until they reached San Antonio, 30 minutes away.

To the men, it seemed closer to 30 hours, but at last they turned off the highway and into San Antonio and parked in a residential neighborhood, in front of a house. A man came out with a key. He opened the

A U.S. border patrolman and a paramedic aid a young Salvadoran woman who was overcome by heat exhaustion and thirst in the Arizona desert in July 1980 after entering the United States illegally. Because the situation in their homeland is often so desperate, immigrants are willing to take great risks to enter the United States.

U-Haul and peered inside. The 46 men were in bad shape, in need of medical attention, but the driver and his friend refused to find it for them. Instead they informed the men they must wait inside the house. The pair then drove away.

The Mexicans were desperate for help. Some staggered into the house. Others, dazed by the harrowing journey, stumbled about the neighborhood. A few dropped in their tracks and fell unconscious outside a home owned by a family of Anglos (non-Hispanic white Americans). The owner, alarmed by the sight of unfamiliar Mexicans sleeping on his lawn, phoned the police. They arrived and arrested 33 of the men, who were deported to Mexico. The remaining 13 were hospitalized; 3 died.

In this photograph from 1963, a border patrolman trains his binoculars on the Rio Grande, the river on the Texas-Mexico border that many immigrants use to enter the United States. In the 1990s, the Border Patrol is as likely to use sophisticated computers, radars, and sensors as binoculars.

Why did these young men go to such extremes to enter the United States? Why could they not enter openly, by the light of day? The answer is that the United States has immigration laws that limit the number of foreigners permitted to live here permanently. Each year, some are allowed to settle here, but they need qualifications that these men lacked. Their only choice was to sneak in—to enter the Promised Land as undocumented, or illegal, aliens.

Mexicans are not the only residents of foreign countries who want to move to the United States and not the only ones kept out. Current immigration laws, established by Congress in 1965, limit the number of people who can enter the country each year. These laws, unlike others enacted long ago, were not designed just to keep foreigners out. The main motive behind them is economic. Our leaders believe the country's economy cannot support an unlimited supply of newcomers.

None of this has crushed the desire of many people to come to the United States. Nor are the immigration laws blindly obeyed. In fact, the laws need full-time enforcing. The Immigration and Naturalization Service (INS), a federal agency located in the Department of Justice, patrols the borders with Mexico and Canada and conducts raids on employers known to hire illegal aliens.

The United States has long shone as a beacon to peoples of other lands. This is as true today as ever before. But because the laws limiting immigration are stricter than in some earlier times, a growing number of people slip quietly over the border, risking deportation or imprisonment. It is impossible to count the total number of illegals in the United States—for the obvious reason that they keep a low profile. But in the 1980s, as many as 10 million undocumented aliens may have entered the country.

Once they arrive, hostility often awaits them. Employers abuse them; their neighbors distrust them.

And they meet with public disfavor. Labor leaders fault them for costing American workers their jobs, for lowering wage scales, and for disrupting efforts to organize unions. Environmental organizations blame them for overpopulating the country and for taxing national resources. Others claim they carry diseases and put a strain on social services. The rash of complaints has led the United States Congress to enlarge the INS budget and to penalize employers caught hiring illegals. But these measures have not had much impact. Today, illegal immigration remains an extremely controversial issue.

It "remains" so because it is, in fact, a longstanding issue, more than a century old. Illegal aliens have poured into the United States ever since the first immigration restrictions were enacted in 1882. These were meant to keep out Chinese laborers who were settling in western states and who continued to do so even after they were declared illegal. In the 1920s, revised restrictions clamped down on southern and eastern Europeans, who, again, sneaked in by the boatload. The 1940s and 1950s saw the first really large wave of illegal

Nativism is not just a concept from 19th-century American history. This photograph from 1975 shows angry construction workers stopping traffic on the Brooklyn Bridge to protest layoffs in the construction industry. Several are carrying signs expressing their belief that illegal immigrants are taking American jobs, a sentiment that dates almost to the beginning of immigration to the United States.

immigration: poor peasants from Mexico seeking temporary jobs in agriculture. In the late 1960s, a second wave of Mexicans began coming here looking for work, primarily in the cities. They were joined in the 1970s and 1980s by the newest wave of undocumented aliens: illegal political refugees from Haiti, El Salvador, and Nicaragua, and illegal workers from such places as Ireland, Poland, and Israel.

As immigration is part of American history, so is illegal immigration. It is a chapter that is being written anew every day.

A masked family of Salvadoran refugees, illegal immigrants, meets the press in September 1983 at the Quaker meeting-house in Cincinnati that offered them sanctuary. As the number of illegal immigrants in the United States rose in the 1980s, religious organizations often offered their help to the newcomers.

THE OPEN-DOOR ERA

In the early years of the United States, illegal aliens did not exist. Our leaders placed no restrictions whatsoever on immigration—no yearly quotas, no laws excluding specific ethnic groups, no preference systems. There were not even any authorities assigned to monitor traffic coming across borders or into port cities. The gates were open to anyone who could afford the trip. This policy of unlimited immigration is sometimes referred to as the "open-door policy."

Its architects were some of America's Founding Fathers. Thomas Jefferson, Benjamin Franklin, and others wanted to create an ideal democracy, one that granted its citizens full rights and freedoms. Such a democracy, they believed, must extend these privileges to all people—regardless of national origin, race, wealth, religion, or political affiliation.

There were also practical considerations. The young nation boasted vast lands and rich natural resources but was sparsely settled. In 1790, when the federal government conducted its first census, the population totaled a mere 3,227,000 and the population density stood at 4.5

persons per square mile. More manpower was needed to invigorate the economy—to clear virgin forests, to develop farms, to speed the growth of cities, and to provide labor for fledgling industries. National security was another issue. At the time, the United States faced a high risk of attack from Indian nations or from European powers, such as England and France. To fend off such a threat, the country sorely needed to increase its military forces.

The open-door policy was formulated in 1793 when the first American president, George Washington, declared: "The bosom of America is open to receive not only the opulent and respectable stranger, but the oppressed and persecuted of all nations and religions; whom we shall welcome to a participation of all our rights and privileges, if by decency and propriety of conduct they appear to merit the enjoyment." Under the U.S. Constitution, Congress, not the president, was supposed to regulate immigration. But because most legislators agreed with Washington's policy, they let it stand. Thereafter, however, immigration policy would be determined largely by Congress.

The First Challenge

In 1798, the nation's first two political parties, the Federalists and the Republicans, were divided. At issue was the United States's position in a war between France and England. The Federalists, disturbed by France's seizure of American merchant ships headed for England, called for the United States to renounce the alliance it had forged with the Continental power in 1778 and to back Great Britain. The Republicans favored close ties with France, seeing that nation's ongoing revolution as a mirror of the United States's struggle for democracy. The Republicans also recalled that France had aided the United States in its struggle with Great Britain; they believed that it was only right for the United States to return the favor.

The Federalists, who controlled Congress, passed two immigration laws. The Alien Friends Act, enacted in June 1798, authorized the president to deport any resident aliens whom he deemed "dangerous to the peace and safety of the United States." The Naturalization Act, pushed through a month later, stipulated that for an alien to be eligible for citizenship, he or she must have lived in the country for at least 14 years, 5 of them in the state where naturalization was sought. Both were aimed at curbing the French influence in America, but as it turned out, the laws scarcely affected immigration. The Alien Friends Act was never invoked, and after the Republicans gained control in 1801, it was allowed to lapse. A year later, the Naturalization Act was amended: It reduced to only five years the period of residency required for citizenship.

The laws had only one major consequence. They gave the Federalist party an anti-immigrant image, which in the long run helped bring about its demise. In

This political cartoon from the late 18th century shows George Washington and a phalanx of troops trampling their political enemies, chief among them Thomas Jefferson and Citizen Genet, France's minister to the United States. Jefferson was a member of the early Republican party and favored close ties with France, whereas Federalist anti-immigration legislation aimed to limit the French influence in America.

1810, the Federalists had realized their folly and tried to change their image with a new theme song:

> Come Dutch and Yankee, Irish, Scot;
> From whence we come it matters not;
> We all make now, one nation.

But it was too little too late.

The Rise of Nativism

During the first two decades of the 19th century, the flow of newcomers was slowed somewhat by the Napoleonic Wars, a series of conflicts between Europe's great powers—England, France, and Spain. Skirmishes in the Atlantic made sea travel extremely hazardous, and many shipping lines suspended passenger service. In 1815, the wars ended, and western Europeans poured into the United States in record numbers. Between 1820 and 1870, 7.4 million immigrants entered the country, most of them from Ireland, Germany, and Scandinavia, though others came from Holland, Scotland, and Wales. These groups—they would later be dubbed "old immigrants"—coveted the economic opportunities of the frontier and in the rapidly industrializing cities.

At first, the flood of newcomers encountered no opposition. But during the 1840s, some Americans objected to the open-door policy. Industrial workers complained that immigrants helped break strikes and caused overcrowding in urban housing. Social reformers claimed that immigrants worsened urban poverty and crime. "Old" Americans, who traced their lineage back several generations, lamented the "dilution of the native stock." And many Protestants were disturbed by the large influx of Catholic immigrants.

Gradually, the various anti-immigrant advocates merged into groups that called for Congress to pass laws narrowing the way for outsiders. Thus began the so-called nativist movement. The first nativist party, formed on July 4, 1845, was called the American party and its rallying cry was "total rejection of the foreigner."

Its declaration of principles denounced European influences responsible for "poisoning the American system."

The most prominent nativist organization was the Know-Nothing party, founded in 1840s. To this day, it remains one of the strangest political entities in American history. Its members carried on in a mock-conspiratorial way, like the members of a secret boys' club. If an outsider asked a member what the goals of the party were, his only response was "I know nothing." (Hence the party's nickname; its official title was, at different times, the Native American or the American

Armed toughs ride into Baltimore to intimidate voters into casting their ballot for the Know-Nothing candidate for mayor, Thomas Swann, in this political cartoon from the 1850s. Know-Nothings was a nickname for the members of the anti-Catholic, anti-immigrant Native American party.

party.) Insiders identified each other using a special signal—one eye closed and the thumb and forefinger placed over the nose. To join, a person had to be a native-born Protestant and had to swear he would always vote for the candidate chosen by the party.

As eccentric as it was, the Know-Nothing party scored early successes. The party leaders made some shrewd decisions. One was establishing a local power base before stepping onto the national scene. In the 1854 elections, the party placed representatives in state governments in Massachusetts, Pennsylvania, Rhode Island, New Hampshire, Delaware, Maryland, Kentucky, and Texas. Many of the votes came from voters whose loyalties to the major political parties had been loosened by the most important issue of the day—slavery.

Some nativists specialized in political organizing. Others fomented hate campaigns, singling out the Irish, who were a natural target because of their abundance,

Catholic immigrants were the object of prejudice in the United States for centuries, and bigots created an entire body of misinformed lore devoted to the "superstitious" rites and "popish" practices of Catholicism. This piece of anti-Catholic propaganda from the 19th century purports to depict Catholic priests burning Protestant Bibles in upstate New York.

their poverty, and their Catholicism. In the eastern states, where most Irish Americans lived, it was common to see job advertisements that included the statement: "No Irish need apply." This hatred could turn violent. Nativists set fire to Catholic convents, churches, and homes and even assaulted nuns.

And there were riots, full-scale clashes between immigrants and nativists. In 1854, eight people died in Baltimore, Maryland. The next year, 20 perished and hundreds were injured as Know-Nothings battled German Americans on the streets of Louisville, Kentucky. Also in 1855, Know-Nothings killed two Irish immigrants in New York City.

The popularity of the Know-Nothing party peaked in 1856 when it mounted a bid to capture the presidency. Its standard-bearer was former chief executive Millard Fillmore. He polled 874,534 votes and won the state of Maryland—a respectable showing for a third-party candidate. Thereafter it was all downhill for the party. A rift divided its proslavery southern wing and its antislavery northern wing, and within two years, the party collapsed.

Meanwhile, the fever for restrictions on immigration had waned. The open-door policy remained in force in most parts of the country. State governments craved newcomers who could cultivate land and populate cities. The railroad companies wanted them to build the new railway lines in the West and to plant and harvest farm products that could be shipped by rail. And other industries, such as the mining companies in the Rockies and Pennsylvania, needed day laborers.

The First Restrictionist Law

In the 1860s and 1870s, nativism flourished only in one region: the Far West. Sentiment there ran high against a single group, Chinese Americans. Immigrants from China had begun trickling in since the 1840s, driven from their homeland by a series of devastating floods

A trainload of immigrants leaves Chicago for the coalfields of Colorado in this 1870 etching from Harper's Weekly.
Despite nativist sentiment, in the late 19th century the number of immigrants who entered the United States rose dramatically, simply because the rapidly industrializing United States needed men to work.

and typhoons and lured to the New World by the prospect of jobs in frontier towns or gold in the Sierra Nevada. From 1850 to 1880, more than 200,000 Chinese—90 percent of them male—sailed across the Pacific Ocean and settled in California, Colorado, and other western territories. The majority took jobs scorned by whites. In communities with a scarcity of women, such as ranches and mining settlements, Chinese did what was sarcastically referred to as "women's work"—cooking, sewing, and laundry.

But some Chinese lined up decent jobs in industries that also employed many whites. For instance, the Southern Pacific Railroad Company hired Chinese workers to help lay tracks that stretched from the West Coast to the Midwest. Others prospected for gold, silver, and copper.

It was the good jobs that led to trouble. White miners and railroad workers resented the Chinese, who crowded them out of work and accepted lower wages. In 1855, mining union leaders in California persuaded the state legislature to institute the Foreign Miners Tax. This drove Chinese Americans out of the mining business.

Money was one issue. Another was race. Many westerners held that the Chinese could not be mixed

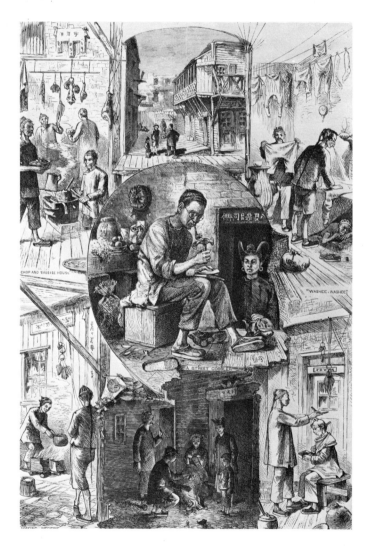

This 1877 woodcut is entitled Life Among the Chinese of Virginia City, Nevada. *In the mining areas of the West, the Chinese often took jobs that involved providing services to the prospectors who had flocked to the goldfields to make their fortune.*

into the melting pot. They were too different, too un-used to American society. But instead of making an effort to include the Chinese, whites took steps to ensure their isolation. In the 1850s, the California legislature passed a series of anti-Chinese restrictions. Chinese Americans were forbidden to enroll their children in public schools, to marry whites, or to testify against them in a court of law.

In the next decade, the Chinese immigration issue dominated political debate in the West. In the 1867 elections, the Workingmen's party, running on an anti-Chinese platform, gained control of the San Francisco municipal government, and the Democratic party used the same tactic to capture all the major offices in the California state government.

Soon the campaign against the Chinese turned violent. In 1871, a mob of whites invaded a Chinese neighborhood in Los Angeles and killed 21 residents. In

Chinese immigrants pose on a handcar on a spur of the Northern Pacific Railroad along the Clark Fork River in the western Rocky Mountains in 1900. It was primarily immigrant labor that built America's railroads.

1876, in an incident that became known as the Truckee Raid, whites torched a Chinese home and then shot its residents when they fled into the streets. More episodes followed, often instigated by the Order of Caucasians, thugs who openly advocated violence. Organized labor also got into the act. The bloodiest incident of all occurred in September 1885, when mine union officials led white rioters on a rampage that killed 28 Chinese miners in Rock Springs, Wyoming. These crimes usually went unpunished. Chinese, after all could not testify in court.

As if this were not enough, West Coast nativists now demanded national action and urged Congress to pass a bill banning immigration from China. Most legislators still shunned nativism, and few were strongly opposed to the Chinese people. But in 1879, Congress passed a Chinese exclusion bill, bowing to pressure from anti-Chinese organizations and making a deal with western lawmakers who promised political favors.

The so-called Committee of 15 was responsible for expelling all Chinese from Tacoma, Washington, in the late 19th century. Similar committees were active up and down the West Coast.

This political cartoon from the 1880s hits at the unfairness of the Chinese Exclusion Act of 1882.

THE ONLY ONE BARRED OUT.

ENLIGHTENED AMERICAN STATESMAN. —" We must draw the line *somewhere*, you know."

No one in Congress spoke up for Chinese Americans. But there was resistance in the executive branch. Officials there held that the bill violated the Burlingame Treaty, a pact the United States had signed with China in 1868. President Rutherford B. Hayes, who did not want to damage U.S.-China relations, vetoed the act. But in 1880, American and Chinese officials renegotiated the treaty and erased restrictions on immigration policy.

In 1882, Congress passed, and President Chester A. Arthur signed, the Chinese Exclusion Act. It barred all Chinese immigrants from the United States for 10 years—except students, merchants, and children of Chinese-American citizens. This was the first time Congress had restricted immigration, and it marked the only occasion in American history that an ethnic group was singled out by name for exclusion. In 1892, the exclusions were extended, and they remained in place until 1943.

Enforcing the New Law

The federal government now had a law against immigrants, but it lacked a method for keeping them out. There were not even complete and accurate records that listed newcomers. In 1819, the U.S. Department of State had begun keeping track of them, but only indirectly—by requiring the captain of every oceangoing vessel that docked at American ports to submit a report specifying the age, sex, nationality, and intended residence of his foreign passengers. A more efficient system was needed.

So, in 1882, the Arthur administration tried to devise one. At first, the task fell to law enforcement officials, borrowed from state governments, under the supervision of the U.S. secretary of the treasury. The officials set up processing stations in major port cities on the West Coast, where they interrogated Chinese seeking entry into the country. All vessels arriving from Asia were required to deliver Chinese passengers to these stations. This lasted until 1891, when the federal Bureau of Immigration was created in the Department of the Treasury and its officers took over the job of inspecting immigrants.

Bureau officers could be ruthless examiners. According to historian Jack Chen in *The Chinese of America*, "Immigrants were asked questions relating to the minutest details of their private life, questions that were often acutely embarrassing, particularly to Chinese women." Agents even grilled merchants and students, who were exempted from the exclusion. Officers obeyed the following instructions: "Make sure that Chinese claiming the right of admission . . . establish the right affirmatively and satisfactorily. In every doubtful case, the benefit of the doubt shall be given to the United States government."

Paper Citizens

Entering the United States was difficult for legal immigrants. It was harder still for illegals. Yet 10,000 or so slipped into the country between 1882 and World War I. They represented the nation's first wave of illegal aliens. Later waves arrived during subsequent years of exclusion (1918–43), but they would be lost in the flood of illegals from Latin America and Europe.

Chinese illegals got into the United States in a variety of ways. A few sailed to Mexico and then crossed the southern border on foot, horseback, or public transportation. This was extremely expensive and time consuming. Others outwitted immigration officials with forged papers that certified them as merchants or students. Still others entered the country legally, as seamen on temporary passes, and then overstayed their allotted time. (This last method was useless after 1898, when the Immigration Bureau first required Chinese sailors to post $300 bonds in order to leave their ships.)

The vast majority of Chinese illegal aliens gained entrance to the country through the "slot" racket. It worked like this: Chinese-American citizens, whose offspring were exempt from the exclusion laws, would falsely report to the authorities that when they themselves had immigrated they had left children back in China whom they wanted to bring over. They then sold the claims of relationship, or slots, to entrepreneurs called slot merchants, who in turn peddled them to workers in China who wished to come to the United States. Those who entered this way became known as "paper sons" and "paper daughters." A similar group of Chinese illegals, called "paper citizens," claimed and received American citizenship after San Francisco's immigration records were destroyed in the 1906 earthquake.

Once they reached the United States, Chinese illegals settled in a number of places. During the 1880s, when riots continued to rock many of the smaller West Coast enclaves, most illegals took up residence in what was then the largest Chinese community in the United States, San Francisco's Chinatown. This well-established community provided a measure of safety from the anti-Chinese riots, but it was a bleak place to live.

San Francisco itself was a thriving metropolis with wide avenues and scores of banks, commercial houses, and opulent mansions. But Chinatown was a warren of cobbled streets and decaying buildings. Almost 22,000 people, 95 percent of them men, were crammed into 12 blocks, most living in rooming houses that lacked adequate baths or lavatories. Crime and vice abounded—particularly gambling, opium smoking, and prostitution—and jobs were limited. Some illegal aliens secured work in local industry. But others joined the *tongs*, violent Chinese gangs that vied for control of the area's lotteries, brothels, and casinos.

In the 1890s and early 1900s, as the anti-Chinese fury died down somewhat, some illegals left Chinatown and headed to eastern cities, such as New York, Philadelphia, Boston, Baltimore, and Washington, D.C. Chinese illegals had better luck there. Many opened restaurants, shops, and laundries. But like their brethren on the West

Terence Powderly, who headed the U.S. Immigration Bureau from 1897 to 1908, was particularly aggressive in enforcing immigration legislation.

Coast, they worried constantly about being apprehended by immigration authorities.

The Immigration Bureau raided Chinese communities with a vengeance between 1897 and 1908, under its chief Terence V. Powderly, the former leader of the Knights of Labor and a founder of the national union movement. Powderly's men seized not only illegal immigrants but also legal ones. On October 11, 1903, officers rounded up every Chinese legal and illegal immigrant they could find in the city of Boston and imprisoned them overnight in two extremely cramped rooms. Out of the 250 Chinese detained, 50 were eventually deported.

No Chinese was exempt from Powderly's raids, not even members of China's upper classes who traveled to the United States for business, travel, or study. Sun Yat-sen, who eventually became the first president of the Chinese Republic, traveled to Washington, D.C., to complain to a congressional subcommittee about being detained by Powderly's men. From 1904 to 1907, out-

Chinese women in detention at the Angel Island immigration station. Through most of the 19th century females—particularly single women—were viewed as less desirable immigrants than men.

raged Chinese merchants and students boycotted American goods.

Chinese legals and illegals apprehended by the Immigration Bureau were held in detention sheds, without bail, while officials debated whether to deport them. This process usually lasted several months. Some Chinese remained in the sheds for more than two years before their cases were settled. Conditions in the sheds were deplorable. Food was scarce, the rooms were dank and overcrowded, and disease was rampant. The detention center on Angel Island in San Francisco Bay was notorious. One social worker who visited the center later reported, "Suicide is common; death is not infrequent."

Today, the white wooden buildings of the Angel Island center still stand as part of the Golden Gate National Recreation Area. Visitors who look at the walls can barely make out poems of lament carved by its inmates while they waited to be released. One poem reads as follows:

> Why do I have to languish in this jail?
> It is because my country is weak and my family poor.
> My parents wait in vain for news;
> My wife and child, wrapped in their quilt, sigh
>   with loneliness. Even if I am allowed to enter this
>   country,
> When can I earn enough to return to China?
> Since ancient times, most of those who leave their
>   homes have not been worth a damn.
> Up to now how many have ever returned
>   triumphant from this battle?

THE DOOR CLOSES

In about 1880, the old immigrant waves began to taper off, and a new influx came from southern and eastern Europe. Italians, Greeks, Jews, Poles, Czechs, Slovaks, Russians, and Hungarians now made up the majority of newcomers.

This happened for several reasons. One reason was developments in transportation. Transatlantic steamships and European railway systems made the trip to the United States more convenient and affordable than before. Another was jobs. As the United States became an industrial power, new jobs opened up in factories, coal mines, and slaughterhouses. Between 1900 and 1912, an average of 1 million immigrants arrived here each year, the peak of the largest influx in American history; a total of 27 million came between 1880 and 1924. Most of these newcomers were uneducated and poor. And most settled in cities in the Northeast.

The Return of the Nativists

The new crop of foreigners aroused fear and contempt among the native stock. Bigotry again reared its ugly head. The new Americans tended to be darker, hairier, and shorter than the northern Europeans who had

Immigrants at Ellis Island in 1900. The great wave of immigration that lasted from approximately 1880 to 1914 consisted mainly of eastern and southern Europeans.

preceded them, and these "alien" characteristics seemed to mark them as members of a separate race. Many old-line Americans complained that the "darker race" would "taint the purity of the national bloodstream." This racist thinking, ignorant as it seems today, was encouraged by certain historians, sociologists, and biologists. Other prejudices had at least some basis in fact. New immigrants tended to retain their Old World customs. They sometimes supported corrupt urban political machines. And, in any case, immigrants were pouring in at such a rate that the population might have trouble absorbing them all.

All this bred a revival of nativism. New political organizations came into existence, including a powerful group called the Immigration Restriction League, which lobbied Congress for a law excluding all immigrants except those from western Europe. Despite the opposition of business leaders, who valued the immigrants as a source of cheap labor, the nativists (now called "restrictionists") pushed several limited bills through Congress. One addressed the fear that foreigners carried infectious diseases and were more apt to commit crimes. Nativists urged the exclusion of persons stricken with "loathsome or contagious disease" and of ex-convicts guilty of "moral turpitude." These restrictions were spelled out in the Immigration Act of 1882, approved by Congress mere months after it passed the Chinese Exclusion Act. The Immigration Act also denied entry to the insane, the mentally handicapped, and those likely to become public charges. Another restriction came in 1885, when lawmakers prohibited private businesses from importing contract laborers. And in 1903, polygamists and political radicals were banned.

These laws kept out only a few thousand immigrants each year. The nativists were not satisfied. In the 1890s, they devised a new strategy. Congress, they claimed, should require all newcomers to pass a literacy test. Publicly they argued that such a test would help preserve the intellectual strength of the nation. Privately they admitted the test would quietly weed out immigrants from southern and eastern Europe, who tended to have less schooling than those from western Europe.

In 1885, Congress passed a literacy bill that was promptly vetoed by President Grover Cleveland. But during the next decade, support mounted for the literacy requirement. Another endorsement came from the Dillingham Commission, a joint congressional-presidential commission established in 1890 to examine the impact of immigration.

The White House would not budge. President William H. Taft vetoed a bill in 1912. So did President Woodrow Wilson in 1915. Both held that stemming the tide of immigrants might cause labor shortages and slow down economic productivity. Restrictionists final-

This political cartoon concerning the United States's attempts to limit European immigration illustrates the low regard in which immigrants were held in some quarters. The sign that the Uncle Sam figure has erected with the aid of a sledgehammer labeled "U.S. public sentiment" likens them to "refuse."

ly prevailed in 1917, when Congress overrode still another veto (again by Wilson). The 1917 Immigration Act stipulated that all immigrants older than 16 years of age had to demonstrate literacy in one language—it did not matter which one. In addition, the bill wove together the various restrictions passed by Congress between 1882 and 1917.

The Asiatic Barred Zone

The 1917 act also capped the campaign to exclude all Asians, not just the Chinese. Like the anti-Chinese agitation, the movement was a West Coast phenomenon led by politicians and labor leaders. Initially the focus of enmity was Japanese immigrants. They arrived only in small numbers in the 1880s and 1890s, and most found work on farms and in restaurants. But they aroused the same racist fears as the Chinese and were branded by politicians and the press as a "dangerous invasion."

Then, in about 1900, more Japanese arrived, and hostility against them grew. In 1905, a coalition of California labor organizations formed the Asiatic Exclusion League and pressed for immigration restrictions. At the same time, a series of editorials published in the San Francisco *Chronicle* argued that Japanese could not possibly "exist peaceably in the same territory as whites."

The controversy boiled over in 1907, when the San Francisco School Board began segregating pupils, putting Japanese and white children in different schools. This enraged the nation of Japan, a formidable power in the Far East. President Theodore Roosevelt persuaded the board to reverse its decision, but he had to promise to restrict Japanese immigration. He issued an executive order in 1907 that forbade Japanese to enter the United States from Mexico and Canada and then convinced Japan to discourage its citizens from emigrating to the United States.

The Asiatic Exclusion League now demanded the exclusion of Koreans, the third sizable group from the Far East. Once again, they badgered President Roosevelt. He in turn struck a deal with Japan, which ruled Korea, and Japan agreed to halt all Korean emigration. Together, the restrictions on Chinese, Japanese, and Koreans excluded virtually all Asians who wanted to come to this country. In 1917, Congress reaffirmed these restrictions by establishing the Asiatic Barred Zone, shutting off the flow of emigrants from a region that encompassed not only China, Japan, and Korea but also India.

The First Comprehensive Immigration Law

The restrictionists scored bigger victories after World War I. Anti-immigration had taken hold nationwide. Labor unions grew vehement, citing poor economic conditions. The return of American soldiers from the war had raised the number of unemployed workers to more than 5 million.

And there were two new factors. One was the Russian Revolution, which resulted in the Russian Communists—the Bolsheviks—taking control of the government. Leaders in the United States, like those in other Western democracies, feared a global Bolshevik plot. In the United States, this fear ushered in the Red Scare, which included government raids on left-wing clubs and newspapers, and political trials that sent several American Socialists to jail. A clutch of nativist groups, notably the 100 Percenters, leapt into existence. The second factor was that, for the first time, large businesses—represented by the National Association of Manufacturers, the Ford Motor Company, and the International Harvester Company—backed immigration restrictions.

In 1921, Congress passed new immigration legislation. The Quota Act of 1921 put a ceiling on immigration, allowing each ethnic group to grow each year by three percent of its population in 1910. The quota favored the most established groups (Great Britain, Germany, and Scandinavia) that already had large populations and stanched the flow from countries (especially in eastern and southern Europe) that had only recently mustered large waves of immigrants. The act also established a yearly ceiling of 357,000 on immigration from outside the Western Hemisphere.

In 1924, Congress tightened the noose further with the Johnson-Reed Act, also known as the National Origins Act. It cut the overall ceiling to 150,000 and reduced each yearly nationality quota to two percent of its percentage of the U.S. population as recorded in 1890. Thus, more than 100,000 places were allotted each year to people from Great Britain, Ireland, and Germany. But Italy, which at the turn of the century was sending more immigrants to the United States than any other country, received a yearly quota of only 5,802. The 1924 act also froze out Asian immigrants. Countries from the Western Hemisphere were exempted from the quotas, primarily because the U.S. government wanted to preserve amicable relations with Canada and Mexico.

U.S. border patrolmen pose with their weapons and vehicles in Texas in the 1920s. The U.S. Border Patrol was established in 1924 as part of the federal government's efforts to restrict immigration.

The Excluded Europeans and the Immigration Bureau

The job of enforcing the 1921 and 1924 acts fell principally to the Immigration Bureau, part of the Department of Labor since 1913. In 1924, the bureau made immigrants register with the government and gave them documents that described their legal status. The bureau also set up the Border Patrol, made up of some 400 recruits who operated out of several bases established on the northern and southern frontiers. The officers were trained in law, investigation techniques, fingerprinting, jujitsu, the use of firearms, and tracking and trailing.

The Immigration Bureau was not an instant success. Its principal task was keeping out European illegals, who were streaming in at a yearly rate of about 40,000. But during the Border Patrol's first 3 years, it ap-

These 15 men were apprehended near Bradenton, Florida, in 1931 as they attempted to enter the United States from Cuba. As the struggle to find work intensified during the Great Depression, immigrants became the target of even greater hostility.

prehended a total of only 12,000 lawbreakers. Many continued to cross the Mexican and Canadian borders with impunity. Others used forged visas or made student visas stand up long after their studies had concluded.

Still others turned to "bootleggers," sea captains who hired two sets of ship crews. The first set included actual sailors who worked aboard the vessel; the others were illegals who paid for the privilege of obtaining classification as seamen. As such, they were entitled to stay 60 days in the United States, long enough to elude authorities and to blend into the landscape. It was a risk, but hopeful immigrants paid up to $1,000 to take it.

Soon the Immigration Bureau grew more efficient. In 1929, officers nabbed 20,815 illegals—the vast majority of them European—and 269 smugglers of aliens. Most were sent back to their homelands. In 1930, the bureau deported 19,000, and another 11,000 left voluntarily. It is difficult to determine exactly how many illegals escaped the dragnet. In 1930, however, the bureau estimated that approximately 100,000 illegal aliens lived in the United States.

Two Grim Episodes

During this period, there was a modest wave of illegal aliens from Mexico. Legal immigrants had begun arriv-

A trainload of Mexicans departs Los Angeles for Mexico in August 1931. During the Great Depression, the federal government and many states enacted comprehensive programs for the repatriation of Mexican immigrants. Most of the deportees had entered the United States legally; many had resided there for a substantial amount of time.

ing from Mexico in the 1910s, but the flow tapered off with the Immigration Act of 1917. Most Mexican hopefuls were poor and unschooled; few passed the literacy test or could afford the eight-dollar head tax. The odds were better if they tried stealing across the border. At first, the risk was almost nil: The border was unpatrolled. Even after the creation of the Border Patrol in 1924, Mexicans still had little trouble. The prime game was still Europeans.

According to INS estimates, about 4,000 Mexican illegals entered the United States each year between 1917 and 1929. Most looked for temporary jobs in the Southwest. Some laid track for the Southern Pacific and Santa Fe railroads. Some picked crops in California and Texas. Some mined copper in Colorado. Few stayed more than a year or two before recrossing the border to Mexico.

In 1929, when the Great Depression buckled the American economy, most Mexican illegals lost their jobs or found themselves targeted by state campaigns to expel aliens. The majority returned to Mexico. The few who stayed later regretted it. Many state governments in the Southwest decided it was cheaper to deport Mexicans than to provide them with aid. In 1930–34, these governments, backed by federal law enforcement agencies, sent more than 400,000 Mexicans packing. Some were not illegals at all but, rather, legal aliens or even citizens of the United States who had lived here for 30 or 40 years.

Meanwhile, immigration slackened. The economy was a shambles in the United States—as it was everywhere else—and few foreigners wanted to come here. But to one group of illegals, jobs were not the issue. These were Jews who fled Adolf Hitler's Nazi regime in Germany. American officials refused to ease German quotas in the late 1930s, despite reports that the Nazis were persecuting the entire Jewish population.

Jewish refugees from Adolf Hitler's Nazi Germany disembark from the liner St. Louis *in Antwerp, Belgium, in June 1939 after being denied entry to American ports. The refusal of the United States to lift its immigration quotas meant that many Jews who might otherwise have been saved perished in Europe during the Holocaust.*

Mexican men say good-bye to their loved ones as the train that will take them to the United States leaves the station. The men were going to the United States to work as field hands as part of the U.S. government's Bracero Program.

LOS MOJADOS

The number of immigrants entering the United States without documents soared after World War II, but their point of origin was no longer Europe. Jobs had opened up there as countries recovered from the war. The new illegals—and they constituted the first massive influx in our history—were Mexicans. This wave lasted until the mid-1950s. Oddly enough, it began with a U.S. government initiative.

The Bracero Program

The American war effort drew thousands of workers off the farm. Some enlisted in the armed forces. Others found jobs in factories, which had rapidly expanded to produce war supplies. The exodus depleted the labor supply in the Southwest, so growers asked the federal government to import temporary help from Mexico. President Franklin D. Roosevelt responded by forming a committee that included the heads of the departments of labor, state, justice, and agriculture.

In April 1942, they settled on a course of action, and American officials sought the approval of the Mexican government. The Mexican leaders hesitated. They needed workers too. They also worried that the laborers

Mexican laborers are processed at the U.S. labor center at Hidalgo, Texas, in 1959 preparatory to their obtaining employment under the Bracero Program. Initially conceived as a wartime measure to ease the labor shortage during World War II, the Bracero Program lasted until the 1960s.

might be mistreated, especially in Texas. Citizens of that state were known for their prejudice against Hispanics. The Mexican leaders remembered the forced repatriation of Mexicans during the 1930s.

In the end, however, Mexico relented, mainly because it saw a chance for their own farmers to learn the advanced agricultural techniques of the United States. On August 4, 1942, the two nations instituted the Bracero Program. It provided for Mexican *braceros* (field hands), to be brought to the United States as seasonal laborers. The program was meant to last only as long as World War II.

In Mexico, officials set up recruiting centers and interviewed applicants. Those who passed muster traveled by train to employment stations in the United States, where officials from the U.S. Department of Agriculture and the U.S. Employment Service assigned them to individual farmers. Employers who participated in the program—most of them located in the Southwest—were required to provide braceros with housing and meals. They also had to cover the workers' transportation costs—from the employment center to the farm and back to Mexico at the end of the assignment. And they were to pay the laborers wages comparable to what American farmers earned. According to the *California Farmer* magazine, it cost a rancher an average of $50 to put a bracero to work. Some 100,000 braceros came to the United States during the war years.

When peace came in 1945, American growers wanted the program extended, pointing to a continuing labor shortage. Of the millions of veterans and laid–off armament workers who needed work, few, said the growers, would accept farm wages. Labor leaders disagreed. They countered that the Bracero Program had kept wages artificially low. Plenty of Americans would willingly pick crops for a decent wage. The growers, who had considerable lobbying power in Congress, persuaded lawmakers to keep the program alive. Mexican leaders did not object. The Bracero Program

A Mexican laborer bundles carrots in Arizona in 1942. Most of the Mexicans who entered the United States in the 1940s and 1950s were peasants from Mexico's central plateau.

served as an escape valve for their nation's unemployed, who otherwise might have stirred up discontent and unrest at home. All told, the program lasted 22 years and brought more than 4 million Mexican workers to the United States. The peak year was 1956, when 500,000 contract workers entered the United States to work on farms in 28 states.

From Braceros to Illegals

The Bracero Program seemed a godsend to poor Mexican farmers. The first temporary workers often returned to their villages with glowing reports about the money available north of the border. Soon the recruiting stations overflowed with applicants. Few passed the screening. In fact, over the 22–year history of the program, only 1 out of every 10 applicants received a contract, according to Miguel Calderón, an official for the Mexican Department of Foreign Affairs.

At the conclusion of World War II, many of the Mexicans whom the United States had recruited as workers were made to return home. These departing Mexicans had been hired as track workers by the Baltimore & Ohio railroad.

For the rejected applicants, the allure of jobs and wealth did not fade. Many were intent on reaping the harvest of the north. In the first decade of the Bracero Program, illegals started arriving in droves. It was the practical thing to do. The recruiting centers sat near the border. It was cheaper to go north in search of possible employment than to take the long bus ride home where no prospects awaited them.

The U.S. government also spurred illegal immigration, though unwittingly. The terms of the bracero agreement stated that participants were to be recruited on Mexican soil. But sometimes American officials found it easier to sign up undocumented Mexicans already living in the United States. Hence it occurred to Mexicans that their chances would improve if they first entered the country illegally and then sought out work. The system broke down in another way. Braceros often were underpaid or overworked. But when they complained to American officials, they got no help. So they skipped—abandoned their employer—and looked for work elsewhere. In so doing, they lost their right to be in the United States and became illegal aliens.

Returning to Mexico, where they would reclaim their rights as citizens, was not an attractive option. The country's economy was in bad shape. Mexico has always been a poor nation. Its land is mostly barren; its mountainous terrain makes transportation difficult; its few rivers do not adequately irrigate the farmland. And these difficulties were magnified by a population explosion. Between 1940 and 1950, Mexico's population grew by a remarkable 30 percent. The weak economy could not possibly keep pace with this baby boom. Unemployment climbed.

Agriculture was especially unpromising. Only 7 to 10 percent of the land was arable, the crop yield was low, and the value of farm profits and wages was constantly undermined by inflation. Farm workers represented an extremely depressed group. They made up 60 percent of the population but took in only 20 percent of the nation's income. In the late 1940s and early 1950s, wages for a single day of farm work in Mexico averaged between 25 and 50 cents an hour. And, as if all this were not enough, a major drought parched the country from 1948 to 1953.

It is not surprising that Mexican farmers and field hands headed over the border. The question is, why had they not done so earlier? One reason is that conditions in Mexico had never been quite so bleak as they became in the 1940s. Another is that conditions in the United States had never looked so good. Just a few years before, during the Great Depression, unemployment in the United States had run almost as high as it did in Mexico. There was a third reason. Not until the 1940s did Mexicans become widely aware of economic opportunities available to the north.

Who Were the Illegal Mexicans?

No one knows exactly how many Mexicans entered the United States illegally from the mid-1940s to the mid-1950s. They made a point of evading the census takers. The only existing records were kept by the Immigration and Naturalization Service as it tried to apprehend

Harsh economic conditions in the homeland convinced many Mexicans to emigrate.

illegals. In 1943, it seized a total of only 8,189 Mexicans. By 1947 the figure reached 182,986; by 1950 it was 458,215; and by 1953 it was 865,318. These figures are not precise. Many illegal aliens were caught and deported only to slip across the border and be caught again. On the other hand, the INS officials estimate that for every illegal entrant they detained, one probably got through. It seems safe to say that from 1942 to 1964 about 5 million Mexicans illegally crossed the border—more than the total number who received bracero contracts.

The illegals of this period were usually called wetbacks, or in Spanish, *mojados*, because so many swam across the Rio Grande, whose twisting path forms the border between Texas and Mexico. In fact, the majority of undocumented Mexicans never dipped a foot in the river. And in later years, wetback and mojado came to be considered racial slurs.

Who were these illegal Mexican immigrants? For the most part braceros, who tended to be single males between the ages of 17 and 22. Most grew up in rural communities of 2,500 or fewer and belonged to the class of *jornaleros* (landless farmhands). And most came from states located on Mexico's densely populated central plateau. Guanajuato was one such state. Others were Michoacán and Jalisco. Emigrants from these places reached the border by means of an extensive network of buses and trains.

These young men usually lacked formal schooling. They could not read or write, they spoke no English, and they knew nothing about American culture. But they were certainly not the poorest Mexican citizens, or the least enterprising. They had enough money and courage to make the long, hazardous journey to the United States. As a *New York Times* reporter wrote in 1954, "It takes more than ordinary initiative to marshal a grubstake, get to the border, and run the Border Patrol's gauntlet, all for the purpose of working harder and at lower wages than most United States citizens will accept."

Crossing the Border

The U.S.-Mexican border runs for 1,900 miles, from the Pacific beaches of San Diego, California, to the Gulf coast of Brownsville, Texas. For most Mexicans, the journey across this threshold began in one of the Mexican border towns. There they learned about job openings in the north and received guidance on avoiding the Border Patrol.

In March 1954 immigration inspector Richard McCowan caught Felipe Ramírez-Pérez as he attempted to sneak across the border near San Diego under the hood of an automobile.

Those who could afford it paid $150 or more to hitch rides in the automobiles of professional smugglers. Others stowed away on boxcars, empty tank cars, and flatcars loaded with steel. The majority simply walked. The most popular routes linked paired cities that faced each other across the divide of the border. There are a dozen such pairs, including Tijuana and San Diego; Mexicali, Mexico, and Calexico, California; Nogales, Mexico, and Nogales, Arizona; Ciudad Juárez, Mexico, and El Paso, Texas; Nuevo Laredo, Mexico, and Laredo, Texas; and Matamoros, Mexico, and Brownsville, Texas. Trails also ran through rugged mountains and remote deserts.

No matter where they chose to cross, danger lurked. If they took circuitous routes through the back country, they faced sweltering heat during the day and bone-chilling cold at night. They also ran the risk of getting lost and running out of food and water. If they crossed into Texas, they had to ford the Rio Grande, whose currents were treacherous in some places and in some seasons. Many areas of the border were patrolled by vicious gangs, who robbed and sometimes killed illegal Mexican immigrants.

Outside major cities, they came up against barbed-wire fences erected by the INS. Those with exceptional agility simply vaulted over the top. This remarkable feat earned those who accomplished it the title *alambrista* (one who jumps the wire). The title sometimes commanded as much respect as that of *torero* (bullfighter). The less athletic often piled up crates and climbed over the fence or looked for a hole they could slip through. In some locales, Mexicans made a living by cutting holes in the fence and charging their countrymen a dollar to use them or by renting mattresses that could be folded over the top of the fence to protect climbers from the jagged metal of the barbed wire.

Some Mexicans died in the effort to cross the border. The rough waters of the Rio Grande claimed several hundred lives each year. Others died of starvation, exposure, rattlesnake bites, and gunshot wounds. Most were buried in unmarked graves.

Life in the "Promised Land"

The hardships did not end at the border. To get to a southwestern town or city where there might be jobs, illegal Mexican immigrants had to navigate the so-called danger zone, a strip of American soil, 10 miles wide, that ran along the border. Patrol officers were concentrated there and made almost 95 percent of all apprehensions in that area.

Once they reached the city, however, illegal Mexican immigrants were usually safe from capture. But then they had to find work, despite speaking no English and knowing nothing of American customs. Most headed for the large, corporate-owned ranches of Texas, Arizona, New Mexico, and California, which hired hands for longer periods of time than did small farms.

The first step toward such a job involved contacting a labor agent, a private operator who collected a fee from both farm owners and farm workers, often gouging both. These agents found prospects by loitering in town squares and side streets. Some served as crew leaders for the workers they recruited. This meant they negotiated the wages and distributed pay, keeping a large chunk for themselves.

Once the job seeker hooked up with a labor agent, he was bused to his new employer's land and placed in a

The lives of Mexican immigrants in the United States were often difficult. The laborers' quarters on this ranch had running water; many employers did not even provide this basic amenity. The photograph was taken in 1944.

57

temporary work camp. Housing was dismal. A few workers rented small shacks or apartments off their employer's land, but most could not afford this option or were not allowed to by their employer. Sometimes they scooped a hole in the ground, made a roof out of a canvas tent, and flung a layer of dirt and straw on top as camouflage against the Border Patrol. On some farms, accommodations were even more primitive. Workers might live in caves, irrigation ditches, or groves of trees.

The job was as grim as the accommodations. Workers toiled long hours for a pittance. Those employed by growers in Texas were forced to work from sunup to sundown, 7 days a week, for an average wage of 15 cents an hour. Mexican laborers in other states fared somewhat better; they earned an average of 40 cents an hour.

Even so, these workers were often shortchanged. Employers habitually credited laborers with fewer hours than they had actually worked or withheld part of each worker's pay until his services were no longer needed. This prevented them from skipping. Worse yet, sometimes all wages were withheld until the work was completed, and employers then turned illegal employees over to the INS. Undocumented Mexican immigrants also fell prey to merchants who operated general stores on or near farms. They realized Mexican workers were loath to venture into towns to shop, for fear of detection, and overcharged them badly.

It was not only Anglos who mistreated these workers; fellow Hispanics also got in their licks. Mexican-American overseers on southwestern ranches often overworked laborers and underweighed goods they harvested. Mexican-American landlords sometimes overcharged illegals for the use of small wooden shacks. One Hispanic lawyer bilked undocumented workers out of $80 apiece for completing a suspension of deportation request that they could easily have filled out themselves with the aid of immigration officials.

Undocumented Mexican laborers, of course, could not defend themselves. They were not American citizens and thus were not protected by the courts. If they reported farmer abuses, they were usually deported. From time to time, state authorities tallied complaints, but usually for the purpose of adding data to labor reports.

One commentator has written that Mexican illegal aliens in the Imperial Valley represented "one of the most highly concentrated survivals of peonage that have existed anywhere." Others have likened the exploitation of these workers to the treatment of plantation slaves. In one sense, however, they were actually

Even those Mexicans who entered the United States legally and obtained citizenship found it difficult to escape a life of unrelenting work and poverty. Seen here is a Mexican migrant worker and his family in their home in California's San Joaquin Valley in 1950.

worse off: Slaveholders considered their chattel an investment that had to be protected, but a farmer who employed illegal Mexican laborers had nothing at stake and could work them till they dropped.

At the end of each harvest season, most illegals went home to Mexico—with little to show for their hardship. The lion's share of their wages was eaten up by basic necessities, such as food and clothing. What remained usually did not add up to more than $10 or $20. Some spent this meager profit on a few American goods—a new hat, perhaps, or a new tool or two. Others gave it to their families. More often than not the money had to cover loans that had funded the journey to the Promised Land.

Given these harsh facts, why did Mexicans keep crossing the border? One reason is many had no idea what they were getting into. By the time they landed on the farm, they were penniless and had no choice but to work until they could afford the return trip to Mexico. Others knew better but came anyway. Bad as life was in the Southwest, it could be even worse in Mexico. "Some income and some shelter represented a definite improvement over what they had in Mexico," in the

The ramshackle dwellings of Mexican immigrants on the outskirts of Los Angeles in 1930.

words of historian Juan Ramón García. A presidential commission put it more bluntly: "The wetback is a hungry human being."

A Losing Battle

It is likely that most Mexicans would not have risked the journey to the United States had the INS been a more formidable foe. In the war years, the Border Patrol virtually ignored illegal aliens from Mexico, just as it had done during the 1920s. The armed forces depleted Border Patrol's ranks, and those who remained barely managed to perform the department's primary task— stopping agents of America's enemies from infiltrating the country.

After the war, the patrol became more serious about catching and deporting Mexican undocumented workers. It enlarged its fleet of cars and jeeps, purchased airplanes to do aerial reconnaissance, and increased patrols of railroad and highway routes leading from the border to American cities. Officers built sand and dirt "track roads" near and across popular trails and examined them for footprints. A Border Patrol division headquartered in El Centro, California, stemmed the flow of illegals into the Imperial Valley.

But the overall picture did not change much. In 1951, immigration officials conceded to a journalist for the *Reporter* that the agency's activities remained "a sampling operation. Those [we] catch are the most desperately poor, the most recently arrived, the least ingenious of the invaders, and even in those categories many are the beneficiaries of chance."

Why did the patrol do so poorly? For one thing, it was far too small to deal with the massive invasion from Mexico, which greatly exceeded the size of the previous illegal influx. In the 1940s, there had been several attempts to expand the patrol's staff and to enlarge its budget, but they had all been defeated by southern congressmen representing the interests of growers who used illegal Mexican labor. The patrol numbered only 700 in 1950. At any given time, only about 120 of these officers were deployed along the 1,900-mile border.

Another reason was federal immigration laws. These prevented officers from searching private homes for illegals and from patrolling ranch land unless they had evidence that illegal workers were there. Also, some officials told them not to press charges against apprehended illegals. And mixed signals came from leaders in Washington, D.C. At harvest times, agents were instructed by INS headquarters to reduce patrols until the crops were in. On a few occasions, they were even ordered to recruit illegal aliens for use by American farmers. All this dampened morale in the INS. As Gladwyn Hill put it in an article for the *New York Times* "The contest is so one-sided, it is a wonder the Border Patrol has not tossed in the towel long since."

A National Issue

During the early 1950s, illegal Mexican workers became a national concern. Labor leaders blamed them for depressing wage levels, displacing American workers, and retarding efforts at unionization and collective bargaining. Health officials blamed Mexican illegals for increasing the rates of such diseases as tuberculosis and venereal disease. Sociologists blamed them for holding back Mexican-American citizens, who were frequently lumped together with their illegal counterparts.

Other ills were also foisted onto the illegal Mexican immigrants, including soaring welfare costs and higher crime rates. It was widely believed that they helped smuggle illegal drugs across the border. For their part, farmers, backed by a powerful lobby in Washington, pushed hard for preserving the illegal labor supply. They insisted that without the help of Mexican workers they would go broke. The Mexican workers themselves were not included in the growing debate. Few mentioned their suffering. And no one cited the strong contribution Mexican laborers had made to the

American economy as an argument for keeping the borders open.

The controversy mounted, and, for the first time in American history, illegal aliens became a national issue. A flurry of stories appeared in the national press about the so-called wetback invasion and its effects. Most journalists were indignant about illegal immigration; few mentioned the appalling conditions imposed on the workers. Historian Juan Ramón García noted that illegals were usually characterized as "poor, sinister, faceless, shadowy beings who skulked across the border in the dead of night in order to deprive others of their jobs and livelihood."

President Harry S. Truman turned his attention to the wetback invasion in early 1951, asking his Commission on Migratory Labor to examine the issue. The commission's final report, issued in February 1952, sided with the antiwetback forces. It recommended that the Border Patrol be strengthened, that effective penalties be imposed on the employers of wetbacks, and that

These undocumented Mexican immigrants were apprehended in southern California in 1954 as part of the Immigration and Naturalization Service's Operation Wetback.

wages and working conditions on farms be improved to attract domestic labor.

Truman asked Congress to include undocumented immigration while it assembled the 1952 McCarran-Walter Act. Senator Paul Douglas of Illinois proposed an amendment making it illegal to employ illegal aliens. It was opposed, however, by Senator James Eastland of Mississippi, who argued that it would be "unfair" to farmers and "unfair to the Mexicans, because it would eliminate such laborers from the economic life of the country." Eastland had many allies and managed to kill the proposal. The McCarran-Walter Act did stiffen penalties against those who harbored illegals. But it stipulated that employing them should not be considered "harboring." This clause was known as the Texas Proviso.

Operation Wetback

Yet the number of illegal aliens entering the country continued to grow. From 1952 to 1953, the number caught by the INS jumped from 543,000 to 865,000. In August 1953, Truman's successor, Dwight D. Eisenhower, sent his attorney general, Herbert Brownell, to southern California for a closer look. Brownell was alarmed by the abundance of undocumented workers and returned to Washington determined to curb uncontrolled immigration.

In 1954, Brownell persuaded Eisenhower to launch an all-out campaign. Thus began Operation Wetback. It gave INS supplementary funds (from the Department of Justice) and manpower (from local officials). Agents cut a wide swath through the Southwest, staging military-style raids and strategically setting up roadblocks. They rounded up thousands of illegals and carted them off to detention centers to be put on buses and taken back to Mexico. Others, getting the hint, needed no escort.

Undocumented Mexican immigrants board a plane at Holtville, California, for the return flight to Mexico on August 11, 1951. The immigrants were apprehended as part of a crackdown on illegal aliens in California's Imperial Valley by the Immigration and Naturalization Service (INS).

The operation was extremely effective. In 1954, the INS captured 1 million illegals, a large portion of the population. The following year the figure dropped to 272,000; in 1956 it sank to 72,000. In 1957, when the number bottomed at 44,000, the annual report of the INS declared that, "the so-called wetback problem no longer exists. The border has been secured." The storm had passed—or so it seemed.

An INS officer stands guard over a group of undocumented immigrants apprehended near San Diego in August 1980.

MEXICANS: THE SECOND WAVE

In 1964, the tally of undocumented Mexicans was about 35,000. By the decade's end the number had risen dramatically—277,000 illegals arrived in 1969 alone. Ten years later, the number had reached almost a million. And 10 years after that, this second wave gave no sign of slackening.

Causes

Why did the situation change? First, hard times hit Mexico again. There was another population explosion, this time caused by a decline in the death rate (thanks to medical advances) coupled with a high birthrate. From 1960 to 1980, the population more than doubled, from 30 million to 70 million. By the mid-1980s, more than half of all Mexicans were under 15 years of age.

Mexico's economy sagged under the strain. The government made a gallant effort to industrialize the country and to some extent succeeded, but at a cost. Farmhands flocked to the cities, which became overcrowded, and production dropped on the farms they deserted. Although the rate of industrialization was fairly rapid, it could not keep pace with the demand for jobs. Each year only about 150,000 new jobs opened up;

The week before this photograph of a street in Pabellon, Mexico, was taken in July 1987, six of the town's residents had suffocated while attempting to illegally enter the United States in a boxcar.

400,000 were needed. By the early 1980s, the combined rate of the unemployed and the underemployed reached a whopping 48 percent.

Oil seemed the answer. In the late 1970s, the country developed its vast reserves and reaped a windfall. But this drove up prices and did not ease unemployment. In 1982, when the bottom fell out of the oil market, the country faced financial ruin. Mexico devalued the value of its currency, the peso, which in turn eroded the buying power of its own citizens. American dollars—and American jobs—looked more attractive.

So did the country itself, partly because of the communications revolution. Beginning in the 1960s, television programs, movies, books, and magazines reached far more homes worldwide than ever before. The fount of this productivity was the United States. American programs filled about a third of the airtime in Mexico, beaming images of a "land of abundance with a nearly endless quantity of consumer goods," in the words of immigration historian David Reimers.

Mexicans gazed northward. The trouble was the number of legal openings for immigrants had dwindled. Since the late 1950s, the Bracero Program had been targeted by American labor groups, who objected to braceros no less than to illegals; by journalists, by church groups, and by social reformers, who cited abuses suffered by Mexican workers. Growers did not argue. They now had machines that efficiently harvested tomatoes, cling peaches, lettuce, and olives. Mexican leaders asked that the program be kept alive, but in 1964 Congress scrapped it.

The next year, Congress tightened restrictions on permanent immigration. This was not meant as a slap against Mexico. In fact, the Immigration Act of 1965 replaced the long-standing nationality quotas with a more equitable system that allotted each country outside the Western Hemisphere the same number of slots: 20,000. But the law also imposed a new requirement on would-be immigrants from the Western Hemisphere, called labor certification. Hopefuls now had to prove that they had jobs lined up in America. They then had to pass a literacy test and satisfy the other requirements dating back to 1917. The 1965 act also established a numerical ceiling on immigration from the Western Hemisphere—an annual maximum of 120,000.

Mexican immigrants had a tough climb. Few had contacts in the United States, and few knew English well enough to secure an American job in advance. And even qualified applicants were not let in immediately, because of the 120,000 ceiling. Mexicans did secure more positions than any other group in the Western Hemisphere—an annual average of 30,000 during the late 1960s and 40,000 during the early 1970s. Still, every year thousands of qualified applicants languished on a waiting list.

In 1976, Congress amended the laws again. It lifted the labor certification, which should have increased the number of qualified immigrants. But the 120,000 hemispheric ceiling stayed in place, and, worse, a 20,000 annual limit was imposed on each sending nation. This last provision halved the number of Mexican entrants. The 1976 law abolished the first-come-first-served procedure and installed a ranking system:

First preference: unmarried sons and daughters of U.S. citizens.

Second: spouse and unmarried sons and daughters of aliens with permanent resident status.

Third: professionals, scientists, and artists of exceptional ability.

Fourth: married sons and daughters of U.S. citizens.

Fifth: brothers and sisters of U.S. citizens.

Sixth: skilled and unskilled workers in occupations in short supply.

Seventh: refugees.

Those who did not fall into one of these categories rarely made it off the waiting list. By the early 1980s, the backlog of qualified Mexican immigrants exceeded 300,000. Many of them chose to immigrate illegally.

The Second Wave

It is impossible to determine the exact number of illegals who crossed the border between 1965 and 1989. Estimates place it between 12 and 20 million, a range so wide as to be almost useless. It is equally difficult to guess the number of Mexican illegals who lived in the United States at any given time. The most commonly accepted figure is from 3.5 to 5 million.

There is more certainty about who the illegals were, thanks to scholarly studies, news accounts, and government investigations. It is known that in some ways the new wave resembled the first wave. Most were young, single, poor, and uneducated, and they came from small rural towns in central Mexico. Most immigrated to find jobs, and most planned to return to their homeland.

But the new wave was not a carbon copy of the old. The illegal immigrants of the preceding decades had wound up on farms. But mechanization cut into jobs there, so the second generation usually lived and worked in cities. Urban illegals filled a wide variety of occupations during the 1970s and 1980s. In Los Angeles, for example, Mexicans became a staple in the

garment industry, working at strenuous and low-paying jobs. An official from the International Ladies Garment Workers' Union (ILGWU), Phil Russo, claimed in 1978 that Mexican illegals "make up something like 70 percent of LA's garment industry." In San Antonio, El Paso, and other cities along the border, undocumented Mexicans provided cheap labor for electronics firms, toy manufacturers, and office supply firms. Mexican illegals also toiled in restaurants, hotels, motels, and hospitals. They served as busboys and dishwashers in restaurants, as maids and bellhops in hotels, as janitors in hospitals. A sizable contingent remained on the farm. Some growers still considered them essential. Said a California citrus grower in 1975, "It's impossible to get locals or domestics to do this work. . . . We just don't get people coming around asking for farm work anymore."

A female Hispanic migrant worker gathers grapefruit in Florida. Many Mexican and other Hispanic immigrants still find work in agriculture.

Another distinctive feature of the second wave of Mexican illegals was that its members settled throughout the whole United States. In the 1970s and 1980s, large concentrations of urban illegals were located in Chicago and New York. And some illegals made their way to Florida, Idaho, and upstate New York.

In general, life was better for the younger generation than it had been for their forebears. Most dwelled in apartments and houses rather than in squalid camps, and wages were higher. In 1976, two immigration experts, David North and Marion Houstoun, found in their study of 800 apprehended aliens that most had earned at least the minimum wage. In 1980, Chicago's INS office reported that the majority of the illegals it had seized in the previous two years took home more than the minimum wage.

The younger generation had the luxury of existing Mexican-American communities that helped them adjust to the foreign culture of the United States. Newcomers saw Spanish street signs and newspapers and heard the language spoken in stores and shops. Community networks eased the search for jobs and housing. There was an active social life in community centers, churches, restaurants, and bars.

This is not to say Mexican illegals had an easy time of it. In 1979, federal investigators arrested a chicken farmer in Louisiana who had bound two illegals in chains in an attempt to enslave them. In the early 1980s, charges were filed against two growers in Arizona for allegedly torturing several undocumented workers. Some growers used armed patrols and threats of deportation to force workers to accept substandard working conditions. The majority of rural and urban illegals escaped such appalling ill treatment. Even so, they usually earned much less than American citizens who worked the same jobs. And, as always, illegals lacked legal protection.

(continued on page 81)

ACROSS THE BORDERLINE

In the 1980s, approximately 10 million people entered the United States illegally. Undocumented Mexican immigrants, such as these four men (overleaf), often arranged to be transported by raft across the Rio Grande from Mexico to El Paso, Texas.

Although some Mexicans enter the United States through legal border crossings (above), desperate economic conditions in their homeland spur thousands of Mexicans annually to risk the dangers of an illegal crossing. Some undertake daring physical feats, as did these men (above right) who scaled a fence on a bridge spanning the Rio Grande. Others risk losing their money and their life to ruthless guides, who often falsely promise to lead them across the border through vast stretches of arid Texas land (below right).

Even with the help of sophisticated electronic devices (above), the INS has difficulty patrolling the entire length of the 1,900-mile U.S.-Mexico border. Nevertheless, U.S. border patrolmen successfully apprehend illegal immigrants such as these two men (above right), who had attempted to enter the United States through Tijuana, Mexico. Captured illegal aliens, only some of whom are Mexican, are held in INS detention centers such as the one in Port Isabel, Texas (right), while awaiting almost certain repatriation.

The INS (below left) and immigration lawyers (above left) offer help in understanding a bureaucracy that can prove too daunting for the average person. In 1986, the Immigration Reform and Control Act offered legalization for undocumented aliens who could prove that they had lived in the United States continuously since 1982 or earlier. These amnesty provisions relieved the burden of fear and secrecy that dominated the life of many illegal aliens (above).

Restrictive U.S. immigration laws, hostility from U.S. citizens, and the possibility of a life of poverty and fear will never deter citizens of other countries from coming to America so long as it offers them greater opportunities and freedoms than they know at home. These Vietnamese women, originally political refugees, met at Camp Pendleton, California, to celebrate 10 years as U.S. residents.

(continued from page 72)

Women Illegals

In the late 1970s, the INS reported that more than 30 percent of Mexican illegal aliens living in American cities were women. This striking development was explained in part by changes in Mexican attitudes about gender. Some women no longer accepted the traditional roles of housekeeper and child rearer. They wanted jobs and crossed the border illegally to find them. Another factor was economic. As poverty spread during the 1960s and 1970s, more families needed a second income.

Women illegals usually reached the United States by direct routes. Few trekked through the wilderness. Those who crossed into Texas generally did not swim the Rio Grande. Instead they hired men to carry them across. Near El Paso, the banks of the river were lined with strong-shouldered men offering ferry service. An illegal named María Montoya described how it worked:

> You find . . . a man along the river. He puts you on his shoulders. You hold your feet up near his chest. Your clothes will not get wet. He walks across and deposits you on the United States side. You tip him a few cents. And he goes back for another passenger.

Mexican men could be found all over the country, from Los Angeles to New York, but women illegals usually took up residence in border areas. Some had left young children behind in Mexico and wanted to be able to visit them as frequently as possible. Others wanted to test the waters in the Southwest before venturing farther.

Many were attracted by the jobs available in the field of domestic service. In the late 1970s, nearly a million illegal Mexican women worked as maids, most of them in San Diego, El Paso, Los Angeles, and San Antonio. So strong was the demand for maids in the Southwest that the INS often did not hound them.

A border patrolman installs a motion-sensitive sensor near a popular crossing point for illegal aliens. Such devices are then monitored from sophisticated communications centers for evidence of illegal entry.

Mexican maids were often hired through a kind of improvised employment market. They gathered outdoors in a central area of an American city—usually in a plaza, park, or shopping center. Anglos drove by, stopped at the curb, and rolled down their windows. Illegals walked up and presented themselves. Sometimes labor agents matched Mexican women with employers. But this was risky. The INS received many reports about women who were recruited as maids but were then forced into prostitution.

Harder to Get In

The INS gave the second wave of Mexican illegals more trouble than they had given the first. The department had improved its methods of finding and catching illegal aliens. Agents now used highly maneuverable helicopters with powerful searchlights instead of twin-engine crop dusters. On land they no longer drove army surplus jeeps but used souped–up four-wheel-drive maxivans that sped along the border at more than 100 miles an hour. And in 1972, the INS began planting electronic sensor devices along the American side of the border. Developed for use in the Vietnam War, these subterranean devices detected the vibrations of footsteps and relayed the information to computer consoles in Border Patrol offices. The INS had also enlarged its staff; about 300 officers patrolled the border at any one time, up from about 120 during the early 1950s.

Illegals also had to contend with a second law enforcement group, the Mexican judicial police, known as *los judiciales*. Mexican law did not prohibit crossing the border. But in the 1970s, judiciales began patrolling border regions, detaining people who seemed headed for the United States. It is widely believed that Mexico's judiciales had no interest in prosecuting the illegals or even in keeping them from slipping into the United States; they merely wanted some of the cash they knew each border crosser carried.

The typical procedure was to arrest the "suspect," charge him with plotting to emigrate, threaten to jail him, and hold him in the back of a police car until he agreed to fork over a bribe. Most detainees complied. Those who did not often were severely beaten. This racket was not limited to the border. Sometimes officers assigned to regions deep in the Mexican interior pulled over public buses heading north and demanded bribes from passengers who seemed to be carrying more than the usual amount of luggage.

Coyotes

As it became riskier to cross the border, Mexican illegals resorted to using coyotes, or professional smugglers. The El Paso branch of the Immigration Service estimated in the late 1970s that close to 50 percent of Mexican illegals relied on coyotes. Their fees ranged from $20 to $2,000. (In 1990 the average was about $600.) In return, coyotes promised to deliver their clients—*pollos* in border terminology—to agreed–upon destinations in the United States. They presented themselves as experts who had special knowledge about the location of INS motion sensors, about the schedule of INS ground and air patrols, about the topography and geography of border regions, and about the habits of the *judiciales*. Coyotes could be found scaring up business in just about every Mexican border town—in plazas, at bus stations, and at popular crossing spots, such as the bridges across the Rio Grande near El Paso.

Coyotes had various techniques for getting their clients across the border. Some led them by foot at night, others hid them in the back of vans and drove across, and some ferried them over the Rio Grande in *lanchas* (small boats). One of the most popular methods involved taking pollos through the "tubes." These are sewage pipes, connecting Tijuana to San Diego, that were built in the early 20th century when the two cities shared a water system. Each tube extends for about a

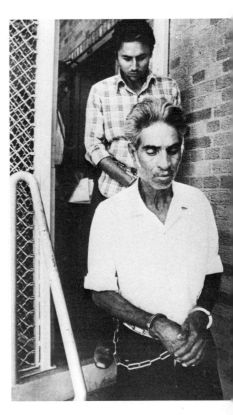

Two suspected coyotes *leave a Tucson, Arizona, courthouse in July 1980. Their clients were Salvadorans who had been abandoned without water in the blazing Arizona desert, resulting in several deaths.*

This drainage culvert runs under Interstate 5 near San Ysidro, California, quite close to the Mexican border. It is often used by undocumented immigrants entering the United States.

mile and is about three feet wide. Crawling through one is a nightmarish ordeal. In the words of a former smuggler named Eduardo Burriaga: "You are on your hands and feet and you fear you'll never get out. It's darker than hell. You can't see, you can't hear, you can only smell. The stench is overpowering."

Some coyotes used a combination of methods. For example, to get illegals from Tijuana to Los Angeles, a coyote might first lead them through the tubes, stash them in a cheap motel (called a "drop house"), and then hire a driver (called a "mule") to convey them the rest of the way.

Much of the coyote trade was controlled by organized networks run by powerful bosses who operated behind the scenes, overseeing finances and personnel while low–level henchmen did the actual work of transporting illegals. Some networks had previously been involved in drug trafficking but turned to smuggling aliens because the risk was lower. American judges tended to give coyotes far lighter sentences than they gave drug smugglers.

Most illegals hired coyotes only to get them over the border. But some smugglers agreed to lead their charges all the way to Chicago and New York—for a higher fee. Sometimes coyotes, like travel agents, offered package deals, which included jobs and housing. Immigration officer William Lucky described such a deal to Grace Halsell, author of *The Illegals*:

> Let us presume a smuggler solicits ten workers for Chicago. He charges $200 to $500 each. Say it's $300. That's $3,000. It includes his services for getting you across the border, and to provide a guide at a pickup point. Once in Chicago, the smuggler will get the aliens a shack—they'll live ten in one shack. The smuggler pays $100 per month for the shack, but he charges each alien $100 per month to live there, so he's picking up another $900 every month. Maybe he's arranged with a work foreman to provide 10 workers at 7 dollars an hour to lay railroad tracks. He gives each alien only 4 dollars per hour and keeps 3 dollars out of every 7 dollars. He's taking $120 off each alien's labor a week, raking off about $4,800 a month plus what he's making on the rent they pay.

Coyotes often showed no sympathy for their clients. In the words of one immigration officer, "Many smugglers are completely amoral. Many former drug smugglers deal with people like they do dope. The have no regard for human lives." Another officer said: "As long as they get their money, the smugglers couldn't care less if the man never finds a job or is half dead when he gets to his destination."

Coyotes were known to lead Mexican illegals to remote areas in the mountains, collect fees, and then desert them. In another common swindle, smugglers promised to arrange jobs for illegals, took payment, and then disappeared. Agents at the INS office in El Paso talked to a group of Mexicans who had paid thousands of dollars to a smuggler in Tijuana to arrange employment for them picking asparagus and strawberries in

Spokane, Washington. When the illegals arrived in Spokane after a 2,500-mile journey, they found no jobs waiting for them and had no way of getting their money back.

Coyotes who transported aliens by truck or van often packed them together like cattle, with lethal results, such as those described in the first chapter. A similar incident took place in 1977. Two INS officers were driving past a tanker truck in El Paso when they heard pounding noises from inside the vehicle. They pried open the tank and found a grisly scene: Two Mexican illegals lay dead on the floor, asphyxiated by fumes, and several others were critically ill. The illegals had been locked in by coyotes.

Violent crimes against pollos occurred most commonly in the backcountry. Halsell describes the experience of a woman named Chula. She, two female friends, and an uncle and his wife hired a smuggler to take them from their hometown in the Yucatán Peninsula to Southern California. They paid $500 each for the

Eighteen illegal aliens died near Sierra Blanca, Texas, in July 1987 while trapped inside this boxcar. The hole in the boxcar's floor was dug by a desperate immigrant in an attempt to get some air.

3,000-mile journey. Everything went as planned until the group reached American soil. Then, in the Otay Mountains, a crime-infested region near San Diego, the coyote turned on them, beating and knifing the uncle and the uncle's wife, and assaulting and raping Chula and her friends. Miraculously, all five survived and reached San Diego, where relatives took them to a hospital.

During the mid-1970s, as coyotes became more of a force, the INS zeroed in on them. In 1976, agents nabbed 9,600 smugglers and three years later caught almost twice that many. Immigration officers scored a major coup in July 1982 when they snared a smuggling boss whose organization had reputedly imported more than 24,000 illegal aliens a year. But these accomplishments made only a dent. Most of those arrested and convicted were dealt minor penalties. Only two-thirds of them were even jailed, and they went back into business as soon as they were released. In any case, these coyotes were mostly petty operators. As one frustrated officer put it, "We catch only the small fry. The big ones always get away."

Domestic Coyotes

In the early 1980s, the INS became aware of a new subset of smugglers: domestic coyotes. These worked exclusively within the United States and helped illegals get from one American city to another, or, in the case of migrant field workers, from one farm to another. Their services were in demand because travel within American borders could be very difficult for illegals. Few could read maps and decipher road signs. Few owned cars. And most shunned air travel. The world of planes and airports was new to them, and they feared their ignorance of it would attract the attention of INS agents.

Domestic coyotes, usually Mexican-Americans, found clients through the grapevine, cruised Hispanic neighborhoods, or visited farms. In *Coyotes*, Ted Conover describes their presence at an Arizona orange farm:

> You knew it was them by the shiny, low-riding American sedans that cruised up to the house, by the radios blaring, by the guys in front wearing mirror shades and just dripping with hipness. Casually, they would light up a cigarette or joint and saunter around or just sit on the hood. The Mexican workers would humbly approach the cars, maybe offer their hands to be shaken, look down at the ground, and stand around for what seemed interminable lengths of time, until one coyote or another revealed what all had known since he arrived: that they could be hired to go to one place or another, that the prices were good but not cheap, that they could leave anytime.

In early 1989, the INS discovered that some domestic smugglers were transporting illegal aliens on board commercial airlines. The agency had for several months received reports from passengers about large numbers of aliens regularly riding on Eastern Airlines Flight 80, which departed Los Angeles every night for New York. Finally, on February 27, agents raided the flight when it stopped in Atlanta and seized 79 illegals. The next day immigration officials plucked 69 more from the same flight before it took off from the West Coast.

Alleged illegal aliens wait to be processed at the Immigration and Naturalization Service office in Atlanta, Georgia.

The agents interrogated the passengers and learned that coyotes had devised the scheme. In exchange for about $1,000, the coyotes had given the illegals one-way coach fare tickets worth $261 and told them how to remain inconspicuous in airports. Flight 80 was considered ideal because of its off-peak departure time—10:50 P.M.

New Ways of Getting In

As the risks of sneaking across the United States's southern border multiplied, some illegals turned to other, newer means of entry. One was the Border Crossing Card, which the Immigration Service began issuing in the early 1960s. The card permitted Mexicans to visit American border areas temporarily, for the purposes of business, entertainment, or shopping. There were restrictions: The bearer could not travel more than 25 miles north of the border, was required to return to Mexico within three days, and was forbidden to use the card to get a job in the United States.

Policymakers in the United States distributed the cards in order to stimulate the economies of American border towns. The idea worked. By the early 1970s, American border towns were getting at least half of their money from Mexican tourists. What American policymakers did not foresee was that the INS would be unable to develop an effective system for enforcing the restrictions placed on card users. Thousands of illegals found they could get into the country for long stints of work.

Obtaining a Border Crossing Card was easy. A Mexican simply had to fill out forms and send them off to immigration authorities. Within six weeks, a card came in the mail. It had the user's name and photo, along with his or her birth date. Illegals used the card in the following way. First, they showed it at a port of entry. Next they traveled to their destination in the United States. Then they sent the card back to relatives in Mexico. This way, if they were caught by the INS, they would not lose the card and could use it again after returning to Mexico.

Countless other members of the second wave of Mexican illegals passed through American ports of entry by presenting false documents. A few used facsimiles of American papers they had fashioned themselves. Others bought fraudulent documents on the black market. For around $500, an illegal could buy a phony version of the Resident Alien Card, usually referred to as the "green card," which certifies that an alien has permanent resident status. For about $1,000, an illegal could obtain a fake American passport and use it to pose as an American tourist or business person returning home from abroad. Authentic American passports—lost by, sold by, or stolen from their original owners and then obtained by document purveyors—fetched as much as $5,000 on the black market.

For much smaller sums, clever and literate illegals obtained American birth certificates (which were accepted as border-crossing documents) directly from state and local governments in the United States. One way they did this was by reading obituaries in American papers, finding a recently deceased American citizen of a similar age, and applying for a duplicate birth certificate in that person's name. In some instances, illiterate illegals paid alien smugglers to procure birth certificates for them. In 1977, the INS apprehended a Peruvian smuggler who, officials alleged, had gotten birth certificates for about 800 Mexicans by posing as an American lawyer representing Texan citizens.

Documents, real and fake, also were useful once illegals reached the United States. With them, illegals could set up bank accounts, secure housing, land jobs, and avoid arrest in INS raids. They also served as breeder documents, enabling illegals to obtain additional forms of identification from state and local governments. For example, an American birth certificate could be used to obtain a driver's license or Social Security card.

These illegal aliens were part of a group of 85 men who traveled nearly 2,200 miles, from El Paso, Texas, to the Bronx, New York, in the back of a tractor-trailer. They had hoped to start a new life in New York; instead, they were apprehended by the INS.

Marrying American citizens was another way in which many members of the second wave of Mexican illegals got into the United States. By marrying an American, a Mexican illegal could qualify for permanent resident status within a matter of months, whereas for nonpreferred Mexicans applying to immigrate, the wait was usually several years.

Some Mexican illegals were in love with the Americans they married. Many others tied the knot expressly for immigration purposes, paying Americans to join them in matrimony. Such "fraudulent marriages," as the Immigration Service called them, cost between $2,000 and $5,000 and were often arranged by smugglers. Couples married in this fashion rarely lived together but, in order to prevent detection by the INS, usually kept the same mailing address.

After 1974, the INS cracked down hard on marriage fraud. All foreign spouses of American citizens applying for permanent resident status were required along with their husband or wife to attend an interview at an INS office. The interviews were grueling, with agents asking each spouse questions about the other that supposedly only legitimately married people would be able to answer. Immigration officers also made surprise visits to couples' homes. Such efforts produced limited results. To apprehend couples for marriage fraud, in essence the INS had to prove that they did not love each other—a difficult task. What is more, the tactic of asking probing questions about suspects' personal lives seemed to violate civil liberties laws.

The Losers

Illegal aliens who were caught were guilty of a crime under U.S. law that was punishable by up to six months' imprisonment, a $500 fine, or both. Defendants were supposed to appear before a judge for a deportation hearing. But such proceedings were costly and time consuming. They involved hours of testimony and paperwork for the arresting officer and required the illegal to be housed in a federal jail. The INS could not sacrifice an agent for a courtroom appearance in every case and did not have enough jail space to accommodate even a fraction of those apprehended.

Thus, 90 percent of Mexican illegals apprehended from the 1960s through the 1980s were allowed a "voluntary return," as the Border Patrol called it. This meant they had only to provide their name and birthplace and fill out a form saying they were voluntarily returning to Mexico. Then they were driven on a bus with other illegals to the border, where an armed guard led them through a gate to Mexican territory and warned them they would face stiffer penalties if they tried to enter illegally a second time.

The few Mexican illegals who were prosecuted usually endured a trying ordeal. Most were forced to wait several months before receiving a deportation hearing. Meanwhile, they sat in one of the four federal detention centers for illegal immigrants—located in Brooklyn, New York; El Centro, California; El Paso, Texas; and Port Isabel, Texas. Conditions in the centers were grim. Brooklyn's, for instance, had no recreational facilities, no library, no common area, no television. Inmates received no new clothes and so could often be found wearing ragged pants and shoes full of holes. Inmates told journalists who visited the centers that they were treated like animals. "I feel humiliated, beaten down, trampled upon," a Brooklyn inmate told one writer.

In an account published in 1978, Grace Halsell described her lunch with imprisoned illegals:

> We sit on wooden benches, jammed closely together, before a long rectangular table. Each man greedily spoons in the food, devouring it as if he hadn't eaten for a week. . . . I do not seem to be among social beings. The human aspect seems

These illegal aliens are being detained in a holding cell in Texas pending processing. Many will probably try again to enter the United States.

submerged by defeat. A man before me looks toil-worn, dazed, depleted. No one speaks. No one looks to either side. I hear only the clatter of steel spoons on steel trays and a greedy chewing and gulping of food.

The INS's stated policy was to hold only illegals who had been apprehended on several occasions. But the service's primitive record-keeping procedures usually made it impossible to tell whether an illegal had a previous record. Each time an illegal was caught, the arresting officer filled out a detailed report in longhand; a secretary eventually typed it on index cards and inserted it in the files of the officer's local station. Such reports never reached other local offices or INS headquarters in Washington, D.C. Consequently, the service had no comprehensive list of previously apprehended illegals. On rare occasions, officers recognized an illegal from a previous arrest or manually located the person's name—provided it was not an alias—in the mountain of files at a local office. Otherwise, they operated on intuition.

The hearings, when they finally occurred, had some severe drawbacks. Illegals were supposed to be given a chance to defend themselves. But few had any idea what was happening. The proceedings were translated into Spanish, but the arcane legal terminology used by the judges was gibberish to the ears of uneducated Mexicans. And no lawyers were provided to assist them. The typical hearing consisted of a judge reading aloud a number of legal documents that he alone understood and then issuing a ruling. In almost 100 percent of cases, the outcome was the same—official deportation.

Like voluntarily returned illegals, deported Mexicans were sent by bus to the border. But instead of being released there, they were put on Mexican buses chartered by the INS and transported into the country's interior. Many were released hundreds of miles from

their homes. The procedure dismayed civil libertarians. In *Los Mojados*, Julian Samora, a professor of Chicano studies at Notre Dame University, asks: "Once an alien is in his own country, what right does the United States have to force him into a Mexican bus for a trip he may not want to take?"

Border patrolman Ed Pyeatt attempts to cheer up a disconsolate young undocumented immigrant awaiting deportation at the border station at Chula Vista, California.

REPERCUSSIONS

The second influx of illegals from Mexico did more than prompt the INS to enlarge its staff and upgrade its methods. It also led to corruption and inefficiency within the agency, and it set off a heated national debate. It was the subject of several bills introduced in Congress. And it profoundly affected life in Mexico.

La Migra's Response

In 1978, and again in 1983, the INS nabbed more than 1 million illegals. But La Migra, as Mexicans called the agency, was a long way from having the problem under control. The Border Patrol had grown by almost 300 percent, yet it remained smaller than the police departments of many cities. Its reach did not extend beyond the most obvious crossing spots.

There were other difficulties. In the late 1970s and early 1980s, the news media and the INS's own complaint division discovered rampant corruption in the agency. Some agents had accepted bribes from employers of illegal workers. Others had seduced female illegals. Still others had let illegals escape from custody—for a fee.

Border Patrol agents at the communications center at San Ysidro use sophisticated electronic equipment to monitor illegal entry to the United States.

Staffing and funding for the INS administrative division had hardly grown since the 1960s. Swamped with work, the INS lost track of thousands of temporary visitors, many of whom long overstayed the expiration dates stamped on their visas. In 1980, Congresswoman Elizabeth Holtzman, head of the House Immigration Committee, called the INS "an agency out of control with nineteenth century tools. Record keeping is a disaster."

The Immigration Service remained concentrated in southwestern border areas even as illegals fanned out across the continent. The INS, powerless to stop this dispersal, reacted with occasional shows of force. During harvest season, they set up roadblocks along major highways, hoping to catch illegal migrant farm workers on their way to new jobs. In cities, they raided businesses suspected of employing illegals. They made headlines on January 19, 1980, when hundreds of agents descended on New York City's Port Authority Bus Terminal and caught 85 illegal domestics aboard buses bound for the New Jersey suburbs.

This raid and others spread fear among undocumented workers. An illegal told the *Washington Post*, "I live with the constant fear they might find me someplace and deport me, send me away. Wherever I go, I have that constant fear. Before, I use to play soccer. I used to go to the Spanish theaters and restaurants. Now I have no place to go."

But the raids netted only a small portion of the illegal population. And they hurt the reputation of the INS. Civil liberties groups repeatedly challenged the raids in courts, contending that they violated right-to-privacy laws. Many Americans believed the INS acted wantonly and showed too little respect for the rights of illegals. The Mexican American Legal Defense and Education Fund, among other organizations, accused the INS of racism. Why, they asked, did almost all its energies go to catching illegals from Mexico, when many illegals

A federal immigration agent (left) escorts a suspected illegal alien from his workplace, a bakery in Chicago, in April 1982. The arrest was made as part of a government crackdown on undocumented immigrants in nine U.S. cities.

come from other countries? The INS replied that Mexicans were easier to catch because of their tendency to enter the country where the Border Patrol was concentrated.

Mexican-American organizations also criticized the way the INS applied its special law enforcement power. Section 287 of the Immigration and Naturalization Act authorized officers to accost and interrogate anyone they wished, without a warrant or probable cause. This made the INS "the only law enforcement agency that can pick up someone and never take him before a judge," said one officer. And some agents used only one criterion in deciding to detain someone—dark skin. This practice resulted in the harassment of legal aliens and citizens of Mexican-American lineage. In San Antonio, Texas; Salem, Oregon; and other cities, Mexican-Americans filed suit.

Government sanctions on illegal aliens also affect documented immigrants. Here, 14-year-old Mario Moreno López (right) is reunited with his brother Oscar in February 1984. Although both Lopezes are U.S. citizens, Mario had been deported to Mexico on suspicion of being an illegal alien.

The Debate Resumes

The general public was also getting interested again in the "silent invasion." In 1972, *US News and World Report* ran a cover story on Mexican illegals. Its headline announced a SURGE OF ILLEGAL IMMIGRANTS ACROSS AMERICAN BORDER. Readers were told, "Never have so many aliens swarmed illegally into the US—millions, moving across the nation." In 1974, a front–page piece in the *New York Times* alleged that more than 1 million illegals were living in the New York metropolitan area.

Interest groups spoke up once more. Labor leaders, health care workers, social reformers, and law enforcement officials all revived the familiar complaints against illegals. They stole jobs, lowered wages, steepened crime rates, smuggled drugs, imported diseases, and drained social services. They gobbled up food stamps, cashed in on unemployment insurance and welfare, crowded hospitals and schools. In 1975, the INS estimated this tax burden at $16 billion. New charges came from advocates of population control and from environmental organizations.

As before, businesspeople defended illegals, maintaining that American workers scorned the jobs filled by illegals. "Picking avocados is damn hard work," said one grower. "Americans work a day or two and drift away; it's easier to go on welfare." And a new force entered the debate on the side of illegals. These were groups, such as the Mexican American Legal Defense and Education Fund, that defended Mexican workers as an important component of the American economy, deserving of protection and benefits.

No one knew just how many illegals there were in the United States. The answer was important: Without it, there was no way to assess the impact of the secret population. In the absence of a certain answer, some people settled for convenient exaggerations. In the early 1970s, the INS placed the total number of illegals within a wide range, between 7 and 12 million. But so

Mexican-American farm workers harvest onions in Arizona. Many immigrants take jobs that better-established Americans are unwilling to perform.

many public officials disputed the figure that the INS commissioned a private consulting firm to make a fresh estimate. Their results were just as vague — between 4 and 11 million. Finally, in 1980, Congress asked the Bureau of the Census to make a guess. The bureau warned that there was little hard evidence to go on but concluded that the population probably fell between 3.5 and 5 million.

Taking Action

In 1972, Congress reopened discussions on illegal immigration. Support grew for a measure that would punish businesses that knowingly employed illegal aliens. A 1977 Gallup poll found that 72 percent of American citizens favored sanctions. But lawmakers failed to enact them.

The obstacle was Senator James Eastland of Mississippi, who chaired the Senate subcommittee on immigration. This subcommittee had to approve all legislation on the issue before it could be voted on by the Senate as a whole. Eastland's constituency included cotton growers who relied on illegal labor. He served their cause by twice crushing sanctions bills that had already passed the House by large margins. This powerful senator stalled hearings until 1976.

Thereafter, Congress was divided by alternative proposals. Some stressed amnesty for illegals; others spotlighted sanctions against employers. Congress haggled over the particulars until 1978, when the legislators established the Select Commission on Immigration and Refugee Policy and told it to deliver a report by 1981.

Meanwhile President Jimmy Carter lobbied heavily for a bill that combined sanctions with amnesty. It died in 1977, and the president tried another approach. He directed the Employment Standards Administration—a federal agency responsible for enforcing labor laws—to

The family of José and Silvia Carmona faced an unusual problem in June 1984. Once this photograph was published in a Kansas City newspaper as part of a story detailing how the Carmonas had won a house, it was only a matter of time before immigration officials determined that the Carmonas were illegal aliens.

form a special task force that would make surprise visits on businesses suspected of hiring undocumented aliens. As it turned out, most businesses they raided were indeed guilty of illegal practices and penalized accordingly. But the small task force could not investigate the vast number of lawbreakers, and most went unscathed.

Individual states also tackled the problem in the 1970s. Twelve passed measures that forbade employers to hire illegals. The laws were rarely enforced, however, and several were even declared unconstitutional. In 1975, Texas barred the children of illegals from its public schools. California tried several solutions. Lawmakers in Los Angeles County banned illegals from using local welfare programs. A few communities would not let illegals into public health facilities except in emergencies.

Effect on Mexico

Between 1940 and 1974, the population of Mexican border cities mushroomed. Tijuana grew from 25,000 to 750,000, Mexicali from 45,000 to 400,000, Ciudad Juárez from 55,000 to 650,000. These cities had manufacturing

Colonia Libertad, a suburb of Tijuana, Mexico, sprawls almost across the U.S. border, which is marked by the concrete post in the foreground at right. One of the ravines in the hills in the background is called Dead Man's Canyon; it is a haven for bandits who lie in wait for illegal aliens crossing into the United States.

plants that drew large numbers of workers from Mexico's interior. But the increases also reflected the rapid growth of the alien-smuggling business and the emergence of the "commuter" population.

Commuters were residents of Mexico who traveled each morning to the United States for work and returned at night to their homes in Mexican border towns. A few had green cards, but most entered illegally, using false papers or sneaking across the border. Each dawn at El Paso, Texas, thousands of Mexican commuters streamed into the United States by crossing the International Bridge, which spans the Rio Grande. The same thing happened at Brownsville and at San Diego, California. According to historian Julian

Squatters' shacks in Juárez, Mexico, just across the border from El Paso, Texas. In the early 1980s, 20 percent of Juárez's population lived in homes like these; nevertheless, Juárez was seen as a haven of prosperity because of the presence of American factories there.

Samora, as many as 400,000 Mexicans commuted to the United States daily in the late 1970s.

The character of life also changed in border towns. More and more would-be illegals drifted in, sometimes stopping there for several weeks. Sprawling camps grew up on the outskirts. People lived in lean-tos tacked together of tin, pieces of wood, or cardboard. A climate of poverty, disease, and crime enfolded the towns as transients, in the hope of scraping together funds for the border crossing, thronged the streets peddling tourist knickknacks, fruit, even their own bodies.

Farther from the border, things also changed. The small rural towns in the central plateau, where so many illegals were born and raised, prospered when these adventurers returned with money. Back home, they bought nicer homes, clothing, and cars. They enlarged their farms and bought more livestock. But the towns themselves suffered. The exodus broke up families and emptied the villages of its most vital inhabitants, as if a far-off war had claimed the able-bodied. In some areas, as many as 7 out of every 10 households lacked 1 parent. Ted Conover spoke to Tómas Cano, a Roman Catholic priest for Ahuacatlan, who said:

> Not since the conquest [the Spanish conquest of the New World] have we suffered such a disaster. ... The husbands—they're all gone, working somewhere else. Sure, maybe their families have more money, but the family! The men come home once a year, they make their wives pregnant, and then they leave again. The wives get so frustrated; "I married a man, not a letter, not a U.S. Postal Service money order," one said to me. The children of these families have a character that is colder than normal.

The crisis in the small towns spread outward. The entire nation grappled with the question. More than one-third of all the Mexican films released between 1977 and 1987

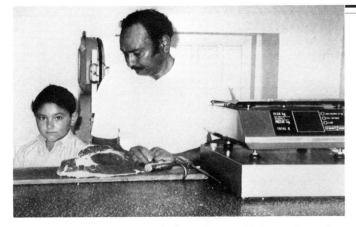

"dealt with intrigues of the border and life on the other side," wrote Conover. Newspapers were clogged with stories about Mexicans living in the United States. Folk songs celebrated the courage and heroism of undocumenteds who made harrowing escapes from the INS, demonstrated remarkable feats of strength and stamina as farm workers, and earned fantastic sums.

There was even a series of novellas devoted to Mexican illegals. It was entitled "Wetbacks: True Tales of the Braceros." Each volume was designed like a comic book, with a glossy cover, color pictures on each page, and balloon dialogue. "Better He Had Never Gone," tells of a young married couple who cross the border in order to support their families. At first, they prosper, but then the wife falls prey to a "loose" American friend, and the marriage dissolves. Later, she dies in a car crash. The cover of the book shows an ominous picture of an INS officer reprimanding a gloomy Mexican. "Hell on Earth" describes the trials of two Mexican brothers. They work illegally in the United States but are cheated by their employers, jailed for crimes they did not commit, and assaulted by fellow prisoners and law enforcement officials.

On both sides of the U.S.-Mexico border, the issue of illegal immigration looms large. Few borders on earth bridge an economic gulf as wide as this one, however, and as long as that is the case, this is an issue that both nations will have to face.

Two Irish immigrants at a meeting of a support group in Queens, New York, in September 1988. In the late 1980s large numbers of undocumented Irish immigrants entered the United States.

THE NEW ILLEGALS

In the late 1960s and early 1970s, Mexicans represented more than 90 percent of all illegal aliens living in the United States. Then the composition of the American illegal alien population began to change. Large groups started coming from other countries. The INS captured illegals from more than 40 different nations and uncovered a new breed of smuggling rings. In 1984, for instance, it cracked a ring whose primary business was sneaking Indian Sikhs from Tijuana into San Diego and broke another (called the Andes Express) that transported illegals from Ecuador to Chicago. By the late 1980s, Mexicans made up only 60 percent of the undocumented population.

Most of the new illegal aliens came from Third World nations in the Western Hemisphere, particularly Nicaragua, Guatemala, El Salvador, Haiti, Colombia, and the Dominican Republic. There were also sizable contingents from two countries in Europe (Ireland and Poland), two in the Middle East (Israel and Iran), and one in the Far East (China).

Many of these illegals came in response to the Immigration and Naturalization Act of 1965. Before it was passed, for example, the Irish had been allotted a large quota of immigrants. But after 1965, the number shrank to only 20,000 people, and by the 1980s, the Irish demand far exceeded this new quota.

For some groups, the 1965 law loosened restrictions. This was the case with the Chinese. By upping China's quota from 2,000 to 20,000, the law opened the door to the first large-scale legal immigration from that nation since the 19th century. This had a snowball effect: Each year's crop of Chinese immigrants reported back to their friends and family about the advantages of life in the United States, and soon more wanted to come than the rules would allow.

Other new illegal groups, such as Haitians and Salvadorans, came for political reasons, especially when, in the 1970s, civil war uprooted millions not only in Latin America but also in Africa, the Middle East, and the Far East. In 1984, immigration experts calculated that the sum of political refugees stood at 13 million worldwide. And the United States accepted three times as many of them as did any other nation.

U.S. Refugee Policy

Politics has always played a special role in immigration policy. Often the doors have been opened to help refugees, despite existing quotas. In the late 1940s and early 1950s, the government admitted more than 500,000 Europeans left homeless by World War II. In 1956, the small quota for Hungary was waived to let in 38,000 freedom fighters who had fled their native land after failing to topple a Communist government. And in the 1970s, the United States welcomed more than 1 million refugees from the Caribbean and Indochina. Most also received medical care, financial support, education, and assistance in finding jobs and housing.

These refugees entered the United States under various ad hoc arrangements—acts of Congress, presidential edicts, paroles by the attorney general. But in 1980, Congress passed the Refugee Act. It welcomed anyone "unable or unwilling to return to [his or her] country because of persecution, or a well-founded fear of persecution, on account of race, religion, nationality,

Chinese seeking visas gather outside the U.S. consulate in Hong Kong in June 1987. The number of undocumented Chinese immigrants in the United States, many of them from Hong Kong, has risen in recent years.

A group of Southeast Asian immigrants attend a meeting of the Commission on Human Rights in Revere, Massachusetts, in September 1985. More than 650,000 Southeast Asian refugees entered the United States between 1975 and 1985.

membership of a particular social group, or political opinion." The act standardized procedures for admitting refugees and authorized the State Department to let in up to 50,000 a year. The president could admit more in the event of an emergency.

Thus, more than 800,000 Cuban refugees have been granted asylum in the United States since 1959, when the Communist government of Fidel Castro came into power. And in 1975, after the U.S.-backed government of South Vietnam fell and its territory was lost to the Communist nation of Vietnam, the United States agreed to admit all refugees who wished to resettle here. By 1985, more than 700,000 Vietnamese had taken advantage of the offer.

But other groups have had tougher luck. The United States refuses refugees from nations with which it is on friendly terms because to do so would imply that the ally mistreats its citizens and damage diplomatic ties. For this reason, in the late 1970s and early 1980s, our country denied sanctuary to refugees from Haiti and El Salvador and classified them as illegal aliens.

Salvadoran immigrants demonstrate in Washington, D.C., in the late 1980s. Undocumented Salvadoran immigrants were usually classified as economic refugees by the INS and deported back to their embattled homeland; the demonstrators were seeking to have immigrants from war-torn El Salvador reclassified as political refugees.

Haitian Boat People

The Haitian exodus was a reaction to the tyranny of Jean-Claude Duvalier ("Baby Doc"), who curtailed civil liberties, denied freedom of the press, and banned labor unions. He crushed dissent with an iron fist through his private army, the Tontons Macoutes. Haitians had grown used to such despotism—in the person of Duvalier's father and predecessor—but matters worsened in the 1970s. At this time, Haiti had the lowest per capita income in the Western Hemisphere. Duvalier asked for foreign aid but then used it for luxuries for himself and other members of the ruling elite. This corruption was common knowledge, but Duvalier's power seemed unshakable, mainly because of the Tontons Macoutes, who arrested innocent civilians, tortured political prisoners, and assassinated rival politicians.

Many Haitians yearned for freedom—in the United States. They did not qualify as political refugees, though, because our government was on friendly terms with Duvalier. Nor did they meet the economic requirement of immigrants. Most were impoverished and had no means of supporting themselves in the new country. So they came illegally. Some were so-called boat people who paid smugglers to ferry them to beaches in Florida.

The journey across the Caribbean was only a few hundred miles, but it was fraught with dangers. Smugglers crammed their passengers shoulder-to-shoulder in rickety wooden vessels that were barely seaworthy. Several boats sank, and passengers went down with them. Another hazard was pirates, who commandeered vessels and robbed, beat, and sometimes murdered those on board. And the smugglers themselves

One hundred ninety-three Haitian refugees aboard their sinking 30-foot vessel await rescue by the U.S. Coast Guard in October 1980. Desperate to reach the United States, Haitian emigrants often attempt to reach the Florida coast in barely seaworthy vessels.

could be treacherous. In August 1979, several Haitians drowned off West Palm Beach after smugglers, hotly pursued by a police boat, forced their contraband overboard.

Some Haitians made it safely. American leaders quickly denied them a blanket parole, such as the Vietnamese and the Cubans had received. Instead, INS officers were ordered to arrest and imprison the boat people. In jail, the Haitians learned that they could individually apply for legal asylum. Most did, with the help of immigration lawyers. But then the State Department announced that Haitians had to demonstrate not only that they had "a well-founded fear of being persecuted" if they returned to Haiti but also that they had "taken a stand in direct contradiction to their government." They had to prove, in other words, that they had openly challenged the Duvalier regime and the Tontons Macoutes. Few had shown such reckless courage.

While awaiting the decision on their individual cases, Haitians were interned in detention camps in the southern United States. Various groups rallied to their side. The National Council of Churches, the Haitian Refugee Center, and the American Civil Liberties Union filed a class action suit against the government. They called for mass asylum and demanded the Haitians be released while their cases were pending. In Congress, the Black Caucus — a group composed entirely of Afro-American legislators — established a task force. It concluded that the government's different treatment of Cubans and Haitians was unfair and perhaps racist. In July 1980, a federal judge ordered the INS to free the Haitians, and President Carter granted temporary legal status to all Haitians who had arrived prior to June 19, 1980.

The boat people were no longer illegal aliens. But their troubles persisted. Unlike the Vietnamese and Cubans, they received no financial support, medical care, or job training. Most were illiterate and unskilled and so struggled to find decent work. Most labored as

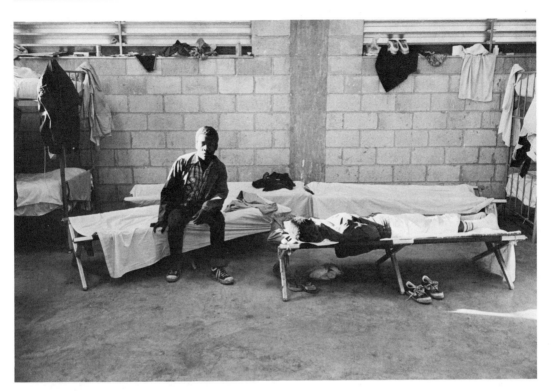

migrant farm workers in Florida in conditions comparable to those of the Southwest in the 1950s.

The boat people were the most conspicuous illegal aliens from Haiti, but they were not the only ones. Others came in as tourists and overstayed their visas, usually settling in Miami or in the Northeast. The largest number went to New York City, where a thriving West Indian community had been established in the borough of Brooklyn. In the 1980s, it was estimated that 50,000 Haitian illegals lived in New York City. Some worked in the garment or service industries. Others were nurses or maids. Others drove taxicabs.

Undocumented Haitian immigrants await processing at the Krone Detention Center outside Miami, Florida.

The Latest Refugees

In the late 1980s, the United States departed from its policy of accepting all refugees fleeing Communist regimes. It refused sanctuary to a massive influx of

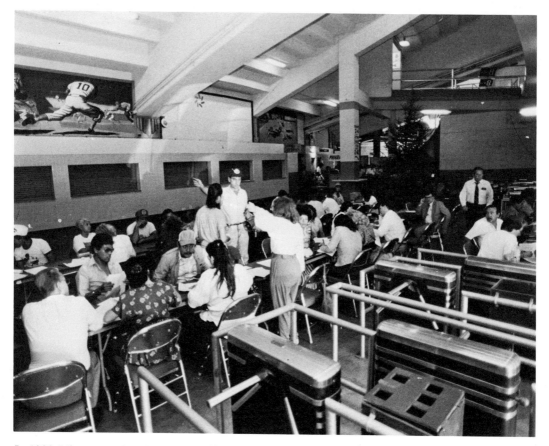

In 1988, Nicaraguan immigrants who attempted to enter the United States without documentation were housed in a minor league baseball stadium in Miami.

illegal entrants from Nicaragua who claimed they were escaping repression at the hands of the Sandinistas.

Large numbers of Nicaraguans began entering the United States illegally in 1987, as economic conditions in their country had deteriorated. That summer, Attorney General Edwin Meese, a fierce opponent of the Sandinistas, decreed that applicants for asylum would no longer be held in detention pending the outcome of their cases. Instead they would be given temporary work permits. Within a year, Nicaraguans were crossing the American border at a rate of 500 a week. Four months later, the flow had risen to 2,000 a week.

Almost 90 percent of the Nicaraguans entered near Brownsville, Texas, the American city closest to Central America. They checked in with the local INS office and filed applications for asylum. Work permits in hand, they traveled by bus to Florida where they joined friends and relatives and looked for jobs. Meanwhile, immigration officials reviewed their cases. This took several months; the INS's asylum unit was understaffed.

The federal government now faced a crisis. Between July and December of 1988, more than 10,000 Nicaraguans had filed applications for asylum. The INS determined most had economic, not political, motives. At the same time, officials in Miami complained that the Nicaraguans were straining the city's social services. Few of the newcomers found work and so ended up on the welfare rolls. The population of homeless Nicaraguans became so large that a shelter had to be set up inside a minor league baseball stadium.

On December 16, 1988, the government established a new policy intended to curb false claims for asylum. Those who applied for asylum in Brownsville had to remain in south Texas while awaiting the outcome of their cases. And none would receive work permits. The INS staff would be increased to handle the mountain of paperwork. The new rules trimmed the number of applications. But the rules also turned the Rio Grande valley into a vast refugee camp filled with tents and other makeshift dwellings with no electricity and water.

Civil rights activists denounced the policy. On January 6, 1989, a group of immigration lawyers, led by Robert Rubin of the San Francisco Lawyer's Committee, filed suit against the government, seeking to overturn the policy. In February 1989, a federal court ruled in favor of Rubin's group and temporarily halted the new policy. But in March a higher court overturned the ruling, and the refugee camps became a fixture along the Rio Grande.

Double jackpot: On April 29, 1989, Justo Ricardo Somarriba, a Nicaraguan immigrant, won Florida's state lottery. Four days later, his request for political asylum was granted, meaning that he and his family would be allowed to remain in the United States.

Near a sign warning that time to enroll in the amnesty program is running out, prospective U.S. citizens wait outside an INS office in Houston, Texas, to have their applications for citizenship approved.

NO EASY SOLUTION

The rise in undocumented immigration from countries other than Mexico spurred efforts in Congress to pass legislation on illegal immigration. In 1981, lawmakers were still split into factions. A compromise was needed. In 1982, Democratic congressman Romano Mazzoli of Kentucky and Republican senator Alan Simpson of Wyoming proposed a measure that united plans for employer sanctions, amnesties, and a temporary worker program. The Reagan administration backed the bill. So did a congressional coalition. The Senate passed the Simpson-Mazzoli compromise bill in 1982 and again in 1983. But it was defeated both times in the House. In 1984, Simpson and Mazzoli steered a version through the House, by the narrow margin of 216 to 211, after the Senate had approved a different version 80 to 20. But when members of the two chambers met in conference to work out differences between the two versions, they disagreed over funding for the amnesty program. Before they could settle the problem, Congress adjourned for the 1984 presidential campaign.

A New Act

In 1986, a compromise law based on the Simpson-Mazzoli bills was finally passed by both houses of Congress and signed into law by President Reagan. The Immigration Reform and Control Act, a landmark in the history of immigration policy, was the first law that primarily addressed the issue of undocumented workers.

From then on, employers who hired illegal aliens were subject to a number of penalties, depending on the offense. A first offender would be fined $250 to $2,000 for each hired illegal. Repeat offenders would face fines of up to $10,000, and chronic violators could be imprisoned for up to six months. The law also required employers to ask all job applicants for documents—such as passports, driver's licenses, or birth certificates—to certify their legal status. (Employers were not, however, to be held responsible for the authenticity of documents.) To answer the charge of ethnic bias, the law called for a new office in the Justice Department to prosecute employers who discriminated against workers "because of their national origins or citizenship status."

The law included amnesty provisions. Undocumented aliens who had lived in the United States continuously since 1982 or earlier could become legal residents. Applicants would have to provide documentation of their years of residence here — such as rent receipts and pay stubs. They could file during a one-year period that began six months after the enactment of the law. Those who qualified would be given status as temporary residents. After 18 months, they would be eligible for permanent resident status, and after 5 years, for citizenship. To prevent a sudden drain on government finances, the law forbade former aliens from receiving many federal benefits for five years, including food stamps and welfare. It also allocated $1 billion to help state governments provide public assistance, public health, and educational assistance to former aliens.

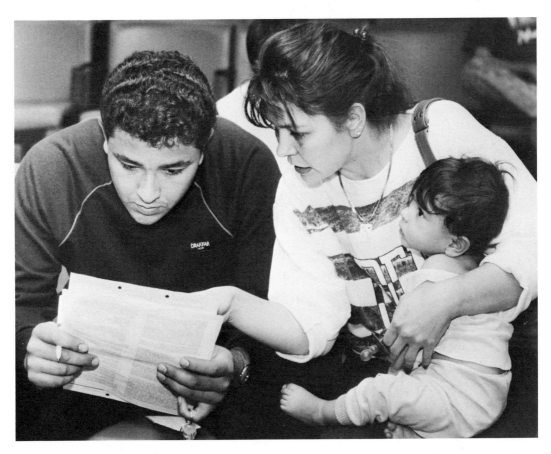

The law featured especially lenient amnesty rules for alien farm workers. They could become legal if they could prove they had worked in American agriculture at least 90 days during the period from May 1, 1985 to May 1, 1986. If shortages occurred, immigration officials were authorized to expand immigration quotas during the years from 1990 to 1993 to let in more field hands.

Finally, the law increased the INS budget from $593 million to more than $1 billion for the fiscal years 1987 and 1988. These added funds were expected to expand the Border Patrol by 50 percent.

The bill had a wide range of supporters. Union leaders endorsed it, as did some Hispanic organiza-

Colombian immigrant Zoraida Naranjo helps her friend Guillermo Galliano with the paperwork necessary to apply for citizenship under the INS amnesty program. Naranjo likened residing in the United States illegally to "being in a big prison."

tions. Raul Yzaguirre, president of a Hispanic organization called the National Council of La Raza, applauded the amnesty provisions as "generous." He said that the bill, "for the first time, provides full rights and protection for both foreign and domestic farm workers." One enthusiastic backer was President Reagan, who believed that it would not only stem illegal immigration but reduce drug smuggling. Another was Bill Bradley, a Democratic senator from New Jersey. He described it as "the most important piece of legislation" produced by the 99th Congress.

The INS claimed that the law had decreased border crossings, based on the smaller number of aliens caught by its officers. The total had dropped 40 percent each year since 1986. Others held that the decline had nothing to do with the volume of illegal border traffic but was probably the result of cuts in the number of Border Patrol officers, for Congress's order in 1986 to expand the patrol was later rescinded.

The main disappointment was the employer sanctions. The sanctions worked, as far as they went. Data showed that 91 percent of a random sample of employers were now obeying the law. The problem was that even a scarcity of jobs did not keep illegals from crossing the border. Conditions were still better than in their homeland. There always seemed to be some kind of work in the United States. Illegals did odd jobs, hawked goods on the street, washed windows, cleaned homes.

In fact, the 1986 law may actually have stimulated illegal immigration, in three ways. First, it prompted thousands of illegals to enter the United States to see if they could qualify for the amnesty with false papers. Second, it gave legal status to a large number of former aliens who still had spouses and children back home. Nestor Rodríguez, a sociologist at the University of Houston, says, "People who came here alone and got papers are now bringing their families here illegally." Third, it strengthened the support network available to illegal newcomers. As Leonel Castillo, former INS com-

On the steps of the federal court-house in Newark, New Jersey, in June 1988, 88-year-old Cornelius Van Veenendaal beams as he displays his citizenship certificate. Van Veenendaal had lived in the United States illegally for 66 years. With him is his fiancée, Jeannie Ryan.

missioner under Carter, explained to the *New York Times* in June 1989, "Illegal immigrants have a long history of following well-established routes and the amnesty program gave those routes a little more solidity. Now, instead of relying on other illegals, a new arrival is likely to know people here who are legal and can offer help with all kinds of things."

Millions of illegal aliens continue to risk their lives to enter the United States. And those who make it continue to live as second-class citizens in a shadow world of poverty and fear. The situation pleases no one. Illegals make more money here than they can at home but are deprived of basic rights that citizens take for granted. American workers resent the continuing competition from illegal aliens for jobs. The INS, given the task of sealing the border without sufficient resources to accomplish that task, suffers from low morale.

Yet it is hard to know what else can be done to improve the situation. Some observers suggest that, given more time, employer sanctions will eventually trim the roster of illegals. Others think law enforcement is the answer. One option is a return to the open-door policy of the past. This might save the government money and reduce hardships for aliens. Another is for the government to pull out all the stops—impose stiffer penalties for employers who hire aliens, throw all apprehended illegals into jail, and thereby force light industry to increase wages to attract American workers to jobs normally held only by illegals. But each of these possibilities guarantees new troubles. For now all that is certain about the problem of illegal aliens is that there is no easy solution.

FURTHER READING

Chen, Jack. *The Chinese of America*. San Francisco: Harper & Row, 1980.

Conover, Ted. *Coyotes: A Journey Through the Secret World of America's Illegal Aliens*. New York: Vintage, 1987.

Crewdson, John. *The Tarnished Door*. New York: Times Books, 1983.

Galarza, Ernesto. *Merchants of Labor: The Mexican Bracero Story*. Santa Barbara, CA: McNally and Loftin, 1964.

García, Juan Ramón. *Operation Wetback: The Mass Deportation of Mexican Undocumented Workers in 1954*. Westport, CT: Greenwood Press, 1980.

Hall, Douglas Kent. *The Border: Life on the Line*. New York: Abbeville, 1988.

Halsell, Grace. *The Illegals*. New York: Stein & Day, 1978.

Johnson, Kenneth A. *Illegal Aliens in the Western Hemisphere*. New York: Praeger, 1981.

Johnson, Kenneth F., and Nia Ogle. *Illegal Mexicans in the United States*. Washington, DC: University Press of America, 1978.

LeMay, Michael. *From Open Door to Dutch Door: An Analysis of U.S. Immigration Policy Since 1820*. New York: Praeger, 1987.

Lewis, Sasha G. *Slave Trade Today: American Exploitation of Illegal Aliens*. Boston: Beacon Press, 1979.

Myers, John. *The Border Wardens*. Englewood Cliffs, NJ: Prentice-Hall, 1971.

Samora, Julian. *Los Mojados: The Wetback Story*. South Bend, IN: University of Notre Dame Press, 1971.

Senate Committee on the Judiciary. *A History of the Immigration and Naturalization Service*. Washington, DC: Government Printing Office, 1980.

INDEX

PICTURE CREDITS

PIERRE N. HAUSER is a New York–based writer and editor who specializes in American history and government. A graduate of Yale University, he served for a number of years as an editor of young-adult books for a New York publishing firm. Before that, he worked as a park ranger in the Southwest and as a reporter for several newspapers in the San Francisco Bay area, including the Pulitzer Prize–winning *Point Reyes Light*. In his spare time, he plays basketball and volleyball and is the drummer for a contemporary music ensemble.

DANIEL PATRICK MOYNIHAN is the senior United States senator from New York. He is also the only person in American history to serve in the cabinets or subcabinets of four successive presidents—Kennedy, Johnson, Nixon, and Ford. Formerly a professor of government at Harvard University, he has written and edited many books, including *Beyond the Melting Pot, Ethnicity: Theory and Experience* (both with Nathan Glazer), *Loyalties*, and *Family and Nation*.